D1549163

REFLECTIONS

REFLECTIONS

Stories for the Junior and Middle School Assembly

Rev. Canon Richard Askew

BLANDFORD PRESS
POOLE·DORSET

First published in the U.K. 1985 by Blandford Press,
Link House, West Street, Poole, Dorset, BH15 1LL.

Copyright © 1985 Blandford Press Ltd

Distributed in the United States by
Sterling Publishing Co., Inc.,
2 Park Avenue, New York, N.Y. 10016.

British Library Cataloguing in Publication Data

Askew, Richard
    Reflections : stories for the junior and middle
    school assembly.
    1. Schools—Exercises and recreations
    2. Recitations
    I. Title
    377'.1   PN4305.S4

ISBN 0 7137 1535 9

All rights reserved. No part of this book may be reproduced or
transmitted in any form or by any means, electronic or mechanical,
including photocopying, recording or any information storage and
retrieval system, without permission in writing from the Publisher.

Typeset by Colset Private Limited
Printed in Great Britain by R. J. Acford Chichester

CONTENTS

ACKNOWLEDGEMENTS

In compiling 'Reflections', I should like to put on record my warmest thanks to all who have helped in research, or in permitting their own stories to be told.

In particular, may I mention my gratitude to the following: Miss Avril Wheeler, the teacher quoted in the Introduction; Mr John White ('Finding Christ under the Surface'), for letting me describe his discovery of the mosaic; the Revd Dick Busch ('How far is it to Bethlehem?') for the story behind a great carol; Mr Edward Smith, C. B. ('The Man for Others') for verifying the problems of underwater steel construction in the London Barrier; Mrs Mary Rowland for telling me the experience behind 'Seeing the Best in People'; Mrs Kathe Wilcox for recalling her childhood memory of a wartime act of courage ('Sharing the Suffering of Others'); Mrs Joan Messenger for researching Smith's Charity ('Giving it Away'); Mr John Dodd for letting me tell his experience ('Time to Serve'); the Revd Pat Ashe, founder of Project Vietnam Orphans (Now Christian Outreach, based in Leamington Spa) for his help with 'It's Better to Light a Candle'; the Revd John Perry, Warden of Lee Abbey, for allowing me to trace the origin of that remarkable community ('One Man's dream'); Major General Wilson-Haffenden — 'Haffy' to his many friends — for permitting me to describe his own part, and that of Brigadier Daniel Perrott, in the miracle of Dunkirk; the Revd John Sewell, Mr Raydon Gowar, and Mr Tom Lenton for piecing together the story of 'Christ the Peacemaker'.

Last but by no means least, may I express my great indebtedness to my former parishioners in the Parish of Ashtead for giving me so much that has gone into these stories; and to my secretary, Miss Mandy Slade, for her care and patience in typing up the text.

Richard Askew
Salisbury 1985

To my best and most faithful critics —
Margaret, Helen, Kate, Christopher and Peter

INTRODUCTION

' "Sit down, stop running round the room. Don't bang your ruler on the desk. What are you chewing? Stop talking and settle down." Within a few minutes the class is quiet, transported to the west bank of the Nile, shoulder to shoulder with Howard Carter in his seemingly futile search for the Tomb of Tutankhamun. A "hidden treasure" story is always a winner. The candle is passed through the hole in the wall of the newly discovered tomb. Lord Carnarvon asks, "What do you see?" and Carter's immortal reply comes, "Wonderful things! Everywhere — gold!" and the class heaves a huge sigh of relief and enjoyment, each student imagining how he would spend the gold if he had got there before Howard Carter.'

In these words one teacher describes the irresistible lure of a good story. And stories can be, of course, not only addictive entertainment, but also a potent medium for communicating truth. When Jesus wanted to depict man's life set in the frame of God's purpose, he chose to do it through stories so powerful as to be unforgettable: it is a psychological impossibility to imagine anyone hearing the story of the Good Samaritan, and then being unable afterwards to remember it!

It is my hope, therefore, that this book contains at least some stories that will stay with their hearers. It is a blend of reminiscences, anecdotes, and scraps of experience distilled over the last ten years from a rich brew of parish ingredients. During that period hardly a term-time week passed without the tantalising opportunity offered by school assemblies for conveying something of the Christian message in words that boys and girls can grasp.

Because these are stories, they need, of course, to be told, and not read, and to be adapted in the telling to the age and awareness of the audience. A biblical reference is given in each case, to be used at the teacher's discretion, if it is felt helpful to relate the theme specifically to the bible in this way, and the thought of each passage is then expressed in a closing prayer.

The material is divided up into two major sections — 'Light for our lives' and 'Mirrors for the light'. The first section seeks to show how Christian insights and principles can illuminate the business of living, while the second picks out particular people in whose lives the light of Christ is clearly reflected. Separating these two main sections is a short interlude, entitled 'Times to reflect', consisting of pieces suitable for marking some of the yearly festivals.

'*Reflections*' will have served its purpose if it provides material that can be used with interest and enjoyment, so that it becomes a part of the hearers' understanding.

1

LIGHT FOR OUR LIVES

WHAT IS GOD LIKE?

Can you draw a picture of your house? Of course you can, and it would be easily recognisable by anyone who knows where you live. But what about drawing mum? That's a bit harder. And if anyone asked you and your friends to draw a sketch of God, the only thing that's certain is that everyone would come up with something different.

This is because you can't see God, and because we all tend to have rather different ideas about him. That's why there are many important world religions. Muslims, Hindus, Jews, Christians and many others all have their own vision of God.

Somebody once told this little story:

> Six blind people visited a zoo and, to their great delight, were allowed into the elephants' enclosure. All of them had been born blind, and none had ever encountered an elephant before. Nobody had ever tried to describe an elephant to them in any detail.
>
> Each in turn was led up to one of the elephants, which was standing very quietly and still.
>
> The first reached out his hand and grasped the elephant's trunk. The second, when it was her turn, took hold of one of the elephant's tusks. The third found its tail, the fourth a leg, the fifth its belly, the sixth an ear.
>
> 'What a strange creature!' said the first. 'It is soft and long, like a huge, thick snake.' (He knew what snakes were like!)
>
> 'No, No!' said the second. 'It's very hard, reasonably short, and with quite a sharp point at the end.'
>
> 'I think it's much more like a thickish rope,' said the third, 'with a tassle on the end.'

'Or a tree', said the fourth;' 'Or a vast cushion,' said the fifth.

'I think it's flat and thin and bendy, like a huge, rubbery leaf', said the sixth.'

You can see the point of the story, and perhaps it teaches us to respect what other people believe about God; maybe they've found something that we've missed.

However, it doesn't at all mean that it's anybody's guess what God is like — just that he's too wonderful for one human being to be able to describe him fully.

Christians believe that God has come close to us and made himself known to us in Jesus. Our best clue as to what God is like is to get as close as we can to Jesus, and learn from him.

John 14: 8–11

Dear Father God,
You are too wonderful and mysterious for us to know you fully.
We realise that men see you
in many ways and through many faiths.
We thank you that, in Jesus,
you have come to us,
and shown us what you are like.
Help us to learn from him.

WHAT DOES THE WORLD LOOK LIKE?

Are you one of those people who always walk along with their eyes on the ground, in case there's something valuable waiting to be picked up? If so, you must love a holiday by the sea, when you can go onto the beach and search along the tide-line, where all sorts of exciting things get cast up. The shore is full of rich pickings for those with their eyes open.

There is a story about a man who walked one day along the sand, looking for whatever he could find. Sure enough, quite soon his gaze fell upon something round and smooth, coloured grey. He stooped down and picked it up, but found that it was only a pebble, though a particularly beautiful and well-rounded one. He looked at it thoughtfully, but could form no idea about how it was made or how it came to be there.

A little bit further on something else caught his eyes, as it lay glinting in the sand. This was a more intriguing find, for it proved to be an old watch in a silver case. Of course, the sea water had got into it, and it wasn't working any more, but it was still very interesting. The man took out his penknife and gently prised open the back. The works inside consisted of an elaborate system of minute cogwheels, each one beautifully fashioned, just right for the work it had to do. As he gazed at this discovery, the man knew that this object had been thought out by a clever mind, and put together with great skill.

Now there are many people who look at this wonderful world and say to themselves that it looks more like the watch than the pebble. That is to say, it seems to them that there is much evidence, in the complicated workings of nature, to suggest that behind it all there is a mind — like a human mind, but much greater and much more clever. That's one of the reasons why people believe in a God: what do you think?

Psalm 104: 19–26

Dear Father God,
what a wonderful world we live in!
How amazing are all the complicated systems of nature,
and the secrets of life itself!
Help us to think about the wisdom and beauty of your world,
and to see you through what you have made.

IT'S A SMALL WORLD

'Seven — six — five — four — three — two — one — blast off!'

How would you feel if you were encased in a space suit, strapped into your seat in a mighty rocket on the launch pad, ready to be shot off into space in a couple of seconds — destination, the Moon? Would you be excited, nervous, thrilled, or just scared stiff?

What did that heroic crew of astronauts feel who were shot into space in the spacecraft 'Eagle' in July 1969 with just that very mission — to be the first men to set foot on the Moon? All went well, and to the delight of millions of people watching and listening back on Earth they landed safely. Then the first astronaut to climb out of the craft took a pace in the dusty soil, and said 'That's one small step for a man, one giant leap for mankind.' After twenty-one hours on the Moon, the crew climbed back into 'Eagle', leaving behind a plaque with these words — 'Here men from the planet Earth first set foot upon the Moon, July AD 1969. We came in peace for all mankind.'

It must have been a thrilling moment for the astronauts to touch down on the Moon: but imagine, too, what it must have been like on the return journey to have seen planet Earth, floating like a little gleaming ball in the sky, dead ahead of them. They must have seen Africa, Asia, India, America, at one glance, and they must have realised that all the hundreds of millions of people on earth — black, white, yellow and brown — are really only members of one great human family. Such a sight would cut down to size all our wars and feuds, all the arguments between countries, and the rivalries between different religions. One astronaut was so moved by catching a glimpse of Earth that he quoted from the first chapter of the Bible, reminding us all of the Christian belief that God made the Earth and all of us in it. 'In the beginning God created the heaven and the earth.' If that is so, we owe it to him to care for one another in peace, and to look after this planet with reverence.

Genesis 1: 1–3

Dear Father God,
You have given us a beautiful world to live in,
and a place in your amazing universe.
Help us to be grateful for this precious gift
and show our thanks
by loving and respecting one another.

BODY AND SOUL

What do you go past on your way to school each morning? How many other schools do you see, for instance, or hospitals, or churches? We take them so much for granted that you probably won't easily remember how many of them you see on your daily journey. If your home is in a town or a suburb, you may see several of each. But if you're out in the country, yours may be the only school for miles around.

If you lived in one of the world's poorer countries, you might have to travel hundreds of miles to find a hospital, and going to school might be a luxury for a few boys and girls rather than something that everybody does.

Take, for instance, the little town of Lui in Southern Sudan. Sixty years ago it was just a village where people lived simply, looking after cattle, growing crops, and hunting animals with a bow and arrow. People knew nothing about the rest of the world, because they hadn't been to school. If they fell ill, they were likely to die, because there were no doctors. They lived in fear of the grim gods of the forest, because nobody had told them about the Christian God of love. And only forty years earlier cruel slave-traders had bought and sold slaves under a big tree on the edge of the village.

Then, in the year 1920, a missionary called Dr Fraser arrived at Lui. He came with his wife and her sister, riding on bicycles, while behind toiled some fifty local men, whom he had paid to carry all his boxes of medical equipment and books.

The chief in charge of the village at Lui didn't know what to make of Dr Fraser. However, the doctor was friendly and said he wanted to help the villagers. Soon after his arrival, a local woman was badly injured by a lion. Everybody thought she would die, but Dr Fraser sewed up her wound and looked after her, and she lived.

After that, everyone trusted the doctor and his family. Quite soon, a little mud-walled hospital was built, and then a school. Every Sunday the missionaries held services under the tree where once the slaves had stood, and told people about the love of Jesus. Before long, one of the boys at the school said he wanted Jesus to become his 'Chief', and so that boy was the first to become a Christian at Lui, and to be baptised under the old slave tree. Soon, many more people became Christians, and the Church in Lui became strong. Then the doctor trained local people to go out on bicycles to the other villages nearby, to preach, to teach, and to heal.

Today, Dr Fraser lies buried near the new, enlarged church in Lui, replacing the little one which he himself had built. A Sudanese clergyman holds services there every Sunday, and very many people come. A few hundred yards away there is a splendid new hospital and a school. Not only that: so great was Dr Fraser's influence that twenty men from that area have themselves trained as doctors, and two of them are now practising in England.

His life and work show us very clearly that the God we know through Jesus cares about every part of our lives — body, mind, and spirit.

Luke 4: 16–20

Dear Lord Jesus,
We know that you went about doing good,
healing the sick,
and teaching people that God is love.
We thank you for Christians today,
who are doing the same work,

and are showing people how to love you,
and how to love one another.

THE LIFE OF MAN

How far back can you remember? Probably your earliest
memory comes from when you were about five years old — a
birthday party, perhaps, or some other family event. It seems
a very long while ago to you, yet in terms of actual years it all
happened not so very far back.

But what about the human race as a whole? What is its
earliest memory? You can read books that were first written
down perhaps, 3,000 years ago, and you can look at ruined
cities and other traces of man that are even far older than
that. Human history goes back a long way: and yet, com-
pared to the history of our planet, man's life has only just
begun.

If you think of it in *this* way you will see just how recently
man appeared on the scene. Take a period of two days —
that's forty-eight hours — and make each of those hours
stand for 100,000,000 years, then you have a scale covering
the whole life of this planet — 4,800,000,000 years!

The first signs of life would not appear until half way
through the first day. It would take another twenty-four
hours for the sea to fill with shelled creatures. By 8 pm on the
second day, fish could be seen, while at 9 pm the first
amphibian would crawl up out of the water. At 11.30 pm on
the second day, mammals would begin to spread across the
world, while at 11.50 monkeys and apes would leave the
trees to explore the ground. Not until 11.59 — one minute
before the end of the whole forty-eight hour period —

would a primate stand upright on two legs and it would take a futher 'half-a-minute' — that is to say, nearly a million years — before man would make his appearance.

So, you see, the human race is still very young. Christians believe that God is behind this gradual coming of age, and that he has a great future in store for us, if only we will let him show it us. He has created us for a purpose, to be the members of his family, with Jesus as our brother.

Psalm 8: 3–5

Dear Father God,
The world is very marvellous and very ancient,
It makes us feel small and unimportant,
and yet we know that we matter specially to you.
Help us to wonder,
and be thankful.

WHOSE WORLD?

What happens if you drop a piece of paper in the play-ground? Does someone tell you to pick it up? Or does it just lie there, along with old tin cans and dirty plastic wrappings, making the place look untidy and uncared for? If so, it's a pity, because your carelessness is being allowed to spoil the place for everybody else.

If you go to the Wildfowl Trust's bird reserve at Slim-bridge in Gloucestershire, you can visit a very lovely spot where many different types of bird can be seen in their natural setting — woods and trees and grassland unspoilt by man. If you look in at the Information Centre in the reserve, you will see these words on the wall: 'Look into the frame below you. You will see a specimen of the most dangerous and destructive animal the world has ever known'. When you look in the frame, you see your own face, reflected in a mirror!

Man is destructive: we do spoil and mess up this beautiful world we have been given by being untidy and wasteful and even by poisoning our surroundings. Whether it's the explosion of a nuclear bomb, or acid rainfall caused by pollution from factory chimneys, it's man making a mess, destroying life and spoiling God's good gift.

Because that's what this world really is — a gift from a good and loving God, who wants us all to enjoy it and appreciate it. We need to remember that and be thankful.

Genesis 1: 26 to 2: 3

Loving Father,
thank you for this beautiful world,
with woods and lakes,
flowers and fruits,
birds and animals.
Help us to give thanks for this abundant gift,
and to respect it.

THE KING'S IMAGE

Have you ever seen somebody with a metal detector walking slowly up and down beside some grassy track searching for buried metal? All sorts of things are turned up out of the soil, their position revealed by the high-pitched buzz of the detector. Often it's just rubbish — perhaps the silver paper off a bar of chocolate, just an inch or so under the surface. But sometimes it may just prove to be something more interesting from the past.

In England, the most fascinating finds are often coins — a sixpenny bit, perhaps, with a picture of King George III on it, found lying under the oak tree where it fell from the pocket of some father of a family as he lay back on the grass and enjoyed a picnic, when the good King was on the throne. There is a chance you might stumble on something much older than that and find yourself looking at the head of a Roman Emperor on a coin that was once part of the house-keeping money of a lady who lived in the Roman villa nearby.

Of course you have to be terribly careful about the way you clean up an old coin. If you try to shine it up with something rough or scratchy, you can spoil the surface completely, and rub away what remains of the lettering and the image.

But if you get a bit of help from an expert and have it cleaned up really properly, then, from underneath all the dirt and the grime, the likeness of some king or emperor will appear for all to see. Even if the design has become a bit damaged or worn with the centuries, you'll still be able to recognise the king's image.

It's a bit like that with people too. God made every one of us, and put a bit of his royal self into each of us. However much people spoil what he made, by being unkind or unloving, however much dirt they smear on to the picture of God within them, that image is still there underneath. And sometimes all the grime can be cleaned away, so that once again people can see the likeness of God shining within their lives.

John 1: 1–5

O God our king,
You have put your royal stamp
on each one of us.
You mean us to be like you,
and in Jesus you have shown us,
what that will mean.
Help us to keep clean and bright
your image within us.

THE PRINT-OUT

Do you enjoy working on a computer? Whether you're
beavering away at school solving complicated mathematical
problems, or simply beating your brother at a game on your
own home equipment, these modern marvels can give you
lots of fun.

But, of course, computers are not there just to amuse you.
They're there to speed life up in all sorts of ways, and to
make business operations swifter and more compact.

Take a word-processor, for example: this is a computer
linked up with a typewriter, which will automatically type
out anything held in the computer's memory. Whole files of
information can be stored away on little floppy discs; there it
can all be kept, unknown and unseen, until, at the push of a
button, when the moment is right, it can be revealed in an
automatic print-out. This brings everything before you,
beautifully typed and clear, so that you can easily understand it.

Perhaps the wonderful way a word-processor works can

help us understand Jesus a little bit better. Just like a word stored away till the right time comes to print it out, so Jesus was stored away as an idea in God's mind till it was the right time for him to be born — God's beautifully clear way of saying something important to us.

John 1: 1, 14

Lord Jesus,
Help us to know that,
in seeing you, we can see God.
You are the Word God uses,
to speak to us and show us himself.
Help us try to listen to you,
and to understand you better.

ONE SOLITARY LIFE

Who do you think has been the most important person in all history? Who has done the most good, or ruled the biggest empire? Who has been known to the largest number of people, or changed more people's lives than anybody else?

Perhaps your choice goes to some king, or president, or general whom you've read about in the history books. Or maybe you think of your favourite pop star, who has sold a million records. Or possibly you favour a TV personality or a top sportsman. Or do you want to settle for the person who invented computers, or Coca Cola?

Somebody once, when they were asked this same question, gave the following answer:

'Here is a man who was born in an obscure village, the child of a peasant woman. He worked in a carpenter's shop until he was thirty, and then, for three years, he was a wandering preacher. He had nothing to recommend him but himself. While still a young man, popular opinion turned against him. His friends — the twelve who had learned so much from him and had promised him their loyalty — ran away and left him. He went through the mockery of a trial, he was nailed on a cross between two thieves and laid in a borrowed grave given to him through the pity of a friend.

Yet I am well within the mark when I say that all the armies that ever marched, and all the parliaments that ever sat, and all the kings that ever reigned, put together, have not affected life upon this earth as has this one solitary life.'

Now, when you come to think about it, that is in fact true. Nearly 2,000 years after his death, Jesus is making some difference, every day that passes, to the lives of at least a third of the human race. And that's something very remarkable indeed. It's enough, just by itself, to make us suspect that there must be something really special about Jesus. What do you think it is that makes the life of Jesus so very special?

John 12: 32

Lord Jesus,
All down the long years of history,
men and women have come to see you
as somebody special;
so special that they have worshipped you.
Help us to see more clearly

just why that is so,
and to know you,
love you,
and serve you better.

WHAT AM I WORTH?

What do you imagine you are worth? Of course, you may be terribly brainy, or immensely popular, or fantastically good-looking, or the best football-player that ever lived: you may be such a splendid person that everyone loves you at first sight, but what are you actually worth? The literal answer, at least in terms of money, is — not much!

There was a well-known writer called Professor Joad who answered the question this way:

'Man is nothing but —
— enough fat for seven bars of soap
— enough iron for one medium-sized nail
— enough sugar for seven cups of tea
— enough lime to whitewash one chicken coop
— enough phosphorus to tip 2,200 matches
— enough magnesium for one dose of salts
— enough potash to explode one toy cap
— enough sulphur to rid one dog of fleas'

Now, if you add together the cost of all those chemicals, our total value wouldn't be much more than a few pounds. So, you see, we are not really worth very much at all.

Or are we? Perhaps the way to find out how much we are worth is not to discover the price of all the bits and pieces that go into making up our bodies, but rather to ask — who loves us, and how much? Your pet rabbit may be very precious indeed, just because you love him. Perhaps we are precious because we matter to those who love us. Above all, we matter because God loves us.

John 3: 16

Loving Lord Jesus,
It's wonderful to know we matter,
because our family and our friends love us.
It's even more wonderful to know that we matter
so much to you that you were willing
to die for us on the cross.

WHO AM I?

Do you have lots of photos showing what you were like when you were very small? It is quite embarrassing to look at a picture of myself when I was only a few weeks old, lying on a rug and not wearing very much at all. Parents always like comparing shots of what we were like at different ages to see the ways in which we have changed and the ways in which we have stayed very much the same.

Actually, there's a great mystery here. My body altered very much indeed as I grew up, but somehow the real person inside me remained 'me' all along. The scientists tell us that every cell in our bodies dies and is replaced once in every seven years or so, but yet we remain ourselves even though our bodies are changing so much. The real 'me' is not the same thing as the body I happen to be wearing for the time-being. It changes, but I don't.

We're always wearing out one body and growing into the next. No doubt mum's always having to buy you new clothes, to replace what you've worn out, and she does that because she loves you and wants you to be properly dressed. In just the same way God, because he loves us, is always giving us a new body. He never stops loving us, and even when, eventually, we leave this life, he's waiting for us in the next, with a special new body for us to wear. He loves us so much he wants us to live with him forever.

2 Corinthians 5: 1–6

Father,
We thank you for the wonder
of how we are made.
We thank you for our marvellous bodies
and the ways in which we change and grow.
Above all we thank you for the real person
inside each one of us,
whom you love,
and whom you invite
to be with you for ever.

FINDING CHRIST UNDER THE SURFACE

John White had a problem: his barn wasn't big enough. Besides being the village blacksmith, he also had a farm with some cattle, and he needed more space to store his bales of straw. So he decided to solve his problem by building a lean-to shed onto the back of his existing barn, to give himself more room.

He got some friends to help, and they began digging a hole to take one of the uprights that would support the roof. They set about the job with a will, but when they had gone down a foot or so, their spades hit something solid. They tried another spot nearby, but the same thing happened. After several attempts, they realised there was an unbroken floor stretching across the whole area, buried under the earth. In mounting excitement they worked hard to uncover it, calling John over to have a look.

Soon a large level surface was revealed, with some sort of design on it. It was John who got a bucket of water and threw it over the floor to clean away the soil. In amazement they gazed down at a complicated pattern, with, at its centre, a head-and-shoulders picture of a young man. Then John realised that what they had uncovered was a mosaic pavement, put together by some Roman craftsman many centuries ago.

Even more exciting was the discovery that the head represented Jesus. On the picture were the Greek letters Chi and Rho, the first two letters in Greek of the name 'Christ'. The mosaic portrait is one of the earliest traces of the Christian faith in the whole of northern Europe.

All this happened in 1963, in the little village of Hinton St Mary, in Dorset. John White saw how important the pavement is, so he let the experts take it up with great care and relay it in the British Museum, where you can go and see it. It provides clear evidence that even in Roman times there were Christians living and worshipping in Dorset.

It must have been exciting to have dug up the soil and discovered the face of Jesus just under the surface. And yet, in a different way, he can be even closer to us than that: Jesus promised to be with his friends forever, and that promise has been proved true right through history down to his friends today. Jesus is there, in the lives of all who love him, making them better people.

John 1: 2–4

Lord Jesus,
We know that you really lived,
in a particular country, at a particular time in history.
We know that you live today
in the lives of men and women everywhere.
Help us to discover you, not just in history,
but also in the lives of other people.

A LOVELY LEGEND

Somerset is one of the most beautiful parts of southwest England. And, in the whole of Somerset, one of the best places to be is the little town of Glastonbury, nestling at the foot of a great hill called Glastonbury Tor. Actually, far back in history, the sea used to come in across the plain as far as Glastonbury and the Tor was a cliff rising from the waters. Now Glastonbury is a peaceful town in the middle of lush countryside, with a park in the centre where you can see the ruins of the old monastery that once stood there.

There's a lovely story told about Glastonbury, and it is this. In the Bible we hear about a rich and generous man called Joseph of Arimathea, who, after Jesus' death, was very kind to Mary his mother, and helped with the arrangements for Jesus' burial.

Now, so the story goes, Joseph did this out of kindness, because he'd known the family a long time. He was a merchant who traded far and wide, and, when Jesus was a boy, he'd actually taken him along in one of his trading ships, which had sailed all the way from the Mediterranean to Britain, and had finally reached Glastonbury.

Because Joseph knew the family of Jesus, he had been very upset when Jesus was crucified, and had done all he could to help. He had taken away the brutal crown of thorns which the soldiers had used to taunt Jesus with, and, later on, when he had to make another trading journey to Britain, he took the crown of thorns with him, and planted it at Glastonbury.

Is the story true? Well, there's certainly a thorn tree growing at Glastonbury, called the Jerusalem thorn; it flowers every year just around Christmas Day, and a flowering branch is always sent off to London, as a present for the Queen. It's also true that a great poet, William Blake, wrote the hymn 'Jerusalem' with this story in mind, and that's why it begins, 'And did those feet in ancient time walk upon England's pastures green?'

But even if this is only a lovely legend, and Jesus in his lifetime never actually came to Britain, what is certainly true is that Jesus, through his Holy Spirit, comes to Britain now, as he does to any other place where his friends are waiting to welcome him into their hearts.

Matthew 18: 20

Lord Jesus,
We thank you for your promise
to come and be with us.
Even though we cannot see you with our eyes,
we can know you in our hearts.
Help us always to make you our welcome guest.

HOW FAR IS IT TO BETHLEHEM?

A man stood one day high up in a tower set on a little hill, in the State of Virginia, USA, looking out over a small town spread before him on the. plain below. At his back was a college, where young men trained to become clergymen and where he himself was a teacher.

Though it was a chill autumn day, the man stood for a long time gazing thoughtfully at the buildings and steeples in the distance. It was getting dark, and, as he watched, the street lamps came on, and one by one the houses also began to glow and twinkle with light.

As he gazed, letting his eyes wander over the scene below, suddenly an idea began to form in his mind. Soon he became so excited by his thoughts that he could stand there no longer, but hurried back to his rooms in the college, and began to write at great speed. Soon, after much had been crossed out and several sheets torn up, the man sat back in his chair and read with satisfaction what he had written: it was a Christmas carol.

The man was Bishop Phillips Brooks, and the carol he had written was to become one of the best known of all carols — 'O little town of Bethlehem'. The town in Virginia which prompted the carol is called Alexandria, and today it is a busy, cheerful, ordinary place, with plenty of shops and even a Macdonalds!

We tend to imagine Jesus as living far away in a special world of carols and Christmas cards, quite unlike our own world. Bishop Brooks imagined Jesus in the everyday world of an American town, and that thought made everything different. Can you imagine Jesus in your town, or in your home?

Luke 2: 4–7

Lord Jesus,
You were born in an ordinary little town,
But you made it special by being there.
Help us to know that you are with us, where we live,
And that you can make that place special too.

WHOSE SHOES ARE YOU WEARING?

Have you ever said something critical about somebody else,
and then felt a bit ashamed about it afterwards, because you
realised just how unkind and unfair you'd been?

Perhaps you teased a boy at school because, whenever he
was asked to read aloud, he did it very slowly and badly: only
later on did you discover that he suffered from the condition
called 'dyslexia', which means that all the letters appear to
him jumbled up and in the wrong order. So you saw that, for
him, to read at all was a major triumph and you'd been really
unkind in poking fun at him just because he read slowly.

Red Indians in Canada and the USA wear beautiful soft
shoes made from skins: they are called 'mocassins' and they
have a very wise saying which goes like this: 'never judge a
man till you've walked a mile in his mocassins'.

The message is clear: we must never be critical about other
people until we know all the facts. But only God knows the
full truth about people: so perhaps we had better leave all the
judging to him.

When God, in the person of Jesus, came and lived
amongst us, you could say he was wearing our mocassins.
He knows all about us and he understands all our difficulties

and handicaps. That's how he's able to forgive us and help us.

Hebrews 4: 15–16

Lord Jesus,
you lived a life like ours.
You know it's hard to be good,
and easy to be unkind and selfish and proud.
Please forgive us
and help us to do better.

TWICE PRECIOUS

What's the most valuable thing you have got?

Why do we rate some of the things we own so highly, while other possessions are less precious to us?

One thing's certain: we are always particularly attached to objects we've made for ourselves. If you have put a lot into something, then it's important to you.

There's a story about a boy who made himself a model yacht. It took him weeks and weeks to finish it, and some of the work was very difficult for him, so that he was glad of a spot of help from dad. But finally the great day came when the boat was complete down to the last bit of rigging, and stood proudly on its stand, glittering in its fresh paintwork.

As soon as dad came home from work, they hurried off together to a large lake nearby, to try it out. It sailed magnificently, beyond their wildest dreams, and for an hour they had a great time, watching it skim across the lake on a tack or a run. Then disaster struck. Just when the yacht was in the very centre of the lake, the wind fell completely, and there the little boat stayed, fifty yards from the shore and quite out of reach. There was nothing they could do but leave it there, with the idea of returning first thing in the morning to recover it.

But when they turned up early next day there was no sign of the boat: clearly it had blown in to the shore, and somebody had taken it. Both the boy and his father were very, very sad, and even dad had a tear in his eye as they turned away from the lake.

Three weeks later, the boy was passing a secondhand shop in his town, when something he saw pulled him up short; there, in the very middle of the window, was his boat, priced £5. He hurried home to tell dad and to ask him what could be done.

'Well,' said dad, 'it's probably not the shopkeepers fault; somebody just sold it to him and he bought it in good faith, not knowing it was stolen. Anyway, we can't actually prove it's yours. There's nothing for it: we'll just have to go in and buy back our own boat.'

And that's just what they did. Ever afterwards that model was doubly precious to the boy, because first of all he'd made it, and then he'd had to buy it back.

Perhaps that's how God feels about his world. It's doubly precious to him; he first of all made it, and it was beautiful and splendid; but then things went wrong, and God's world went far away from him. In the end, to get it back again, he had to buy it at a price, so that it could be his once more. And that price was very costly — nothing less than the suffering of Jesus on the cross. No wonder that God loves us so much.

John 3: 16–17

Father,
we thank you
that first of all you made us,
and then you bought us back,
at such a costly price.
You love us so much: help us to love you in return.

THE MAN FOR OTHERS

Do you like exploring rivers and ponds? If so you have probably tried to cross a stream by stepping on to a tree trunk or a stone, only to find it dipping under your weight. Then you end up with shoes full of water and a good telling-off when you get home.

Something similar but rather more serious is happening to the whole of Great Britain! Believe it or not, the south-eastern part of England is gradually sinking down into the sea, while Scotland and the north-west, on the other hand, are actually rising. Of course, it isn't happening all that quickly — about one foot every hundred years — but that's quite enough to make a difference. In particular, it means that London has been in danger of flooding whenever the tides are particularly high, and the wind is in that direction. So the government has taken a very important step to prevent what could be a terrible disaster: it has built a barrier right across the River Thames to hold back extra high flood tides.

The Thames Barrier is an engineering wonder — a number of massive steel gates stretching more than five hundred yards across from one bank to the other, gates which can be swung shut in an emergency to keep London safe. No wonder it was the Queen herself who came to mark the completion of this vital project in 1984.

But, when you make something out of steel that is always going to stand in water, rust becomes a very big problem. How can you stop the steel gates rusting away? This is how it's done: some metals rust more easily than others — zinc, for instance, rusts very easily. If you put zinc next to steel, the zinc will attract all the rust away from the steel, rusting away itself while leaving the other metal free from rust. So, in the Thames Barrier, wherever there is steel, pieces of zinc are placed alongside, so that the steel does not rust.

Zinc when it is used in this way is given up to save the steel. Engineers call this way of using zinc 'sacrificial'.

Like the zinc drawing the rust away from the steel onto itself, so Jesus, when he gave his life on the cross, drew the worst of punishments onto himself, so that we could go free. That's something very wonderful, and the more you think about it, the more grateful you feel.

John 11: 45–52

Lord Jesus,
it is a great mystery —
your dying on the cross.
But we know it was for us,
that through your death
we might find the secret of real life.
As we grow to understand this more deeply
so help us to become more grateful,
and to show it by the way we live.

BREAKING OUT

How would you like it if men came to your town one day
and started to build a great wall right down the middle of the
High Street? And went on building it, higher and higher, so
that, after a few days, it became quite impossible for anyone
to cross from one side of the town to the other? Think how
terrible it would be, to be cut off from school friends and
perhaps even from an uncle and aunt, or your grandparents.

It's hard to imagine such a thing happening: and yet that
is precisely what did take place in the city of Berlin. In 1961
the Berlin Wall was built, cutting off West Berlin from East
Berlin entirely. It's difficult to understand the quarrel which
lay behind the building of this wall, but it's to do with the
way that the countries of Europe became divided between
those who wanted to become friends with the Russians, and
those who wanted to join up with the freer countries of the
West. The result was the setting up of a heavily guarded
frontier right across Europe from north to south. This frontier came to be called the Iron Curtain, and in the city of
Berlin it actually takes the form of this great wall. It was put
there by the Russians and East Germans to keep their people
in, and to keep out visitors from the West.

Of course, very many people have tried to escape from the
Eastern countries to the free world. They've tried every way
you can imagine to get across that wall. Some have tunnelled
beneath it, others have climbed over it. Heavy lorries have
been driven fast, so as to crash through the gates in it, despite
the guards and the machine guns. One family even made
their own balloon, filled it with hot air, and floated to
freedom high above the sentries below. Many people have
tried to escape but have failed, being shot in the attempt, or
blown up by a mine. There stands the Wall to this day, a

very sad reminder of the way that we human beings just can't seem to get on together.

We all know what it's like, because sometimes, even in the best families, there's a sharp quarrel, and then there seems to be a sort of invisible wall between the different members of that family. You can't speak to each other or get across to each other at all.

If we can cut ourselves off from each other in this way, we can cut ourselves off from God as well. If we do something bad, like being unkind or unfair or untruthful, there seems to be a great barrier between us and God, real enough even though we can't see it. We feel bad about it, but we don't seem to be able to get away from the feeling.

Jesus came to set us free from all that. He doesn't want us to be trapped and shut in by other people, as the East Berliners are, or by ourselves, as we are when we do something wrong. He came to lead us over the great wall put up by our sins into the freedom beyond.

Hebrews 10: 19–20

Lord Jesus,
Don't let us be cut off from one another
by anger and unkindness and lies.
You can help us to break through the barriers
that divide us
because you come to make us friends
with each other and with you.

SEEING THE BEST IN PEOPLE

A clergyman was once visiting the patients in the local hospital. In a single room he came across an old lady who was obviously very ill, being looked after by her husband. She was fast asleep and snoring noisily, and the drugs she had been given had made her grow very plump. The poor old soul was not a pretty sight. The clergyman looked at the couple sympathetically, 'How is she getting on?' he asked the husband, 'Oh, she's doing alright,' the old gentleman replied. Then, looking with love at his wife stretched out asleep, he added, 'Isn't she beautiful?'

You always see the best in people when you can look at them with love in your eyes. Jesus was constantly doing it. He looked at Peter, who was a very unreliable person, often making promises and not keeping them, and he said, 'You are Peter, the man of Rock.' He met Zacchaeus the tax gatherer, who was really a bit of a crook, and he went to call on him at home just to show how much he trusted him. Both Peter and Zacchaeus, through being trusted, immediately became more trustworthy.

If we're going to treat people as Jesus did, then we must get into the habit of looking out for what's good in other people, and not just seeing what's not so good. We've all got a long way to go if we're going to grow into the sort of people we're meant to be. Jesus looked at Peter and Zacchaeus with love and he saw what was best in them. That's how he looks at all of us. What do you think he sees in you?

Matthew 16: 13–19

Lord Jesus,
You always looked at what people could become

and not just at what they are.
Help us to treat other people like that,
by looking for their good points.
And show us what we too might become
through your love.

THE SECRET WEAPON

Do you enjoy films and TV programmes like 'Star Wars',
which give us vivid pictures of the wars of the future,
fought out between brave spacemen and invaders from
other planets? There are always plenty of battles, in which
new and horrific weapons are used. Laser guns blaze out
across space, and the enemy just shrivel up under their
attack.

Of course, these stories are only make-believe, but there
really are inventions today which, if used as weapons, can
pick out targets a long way off and destroy them.

If that's an alarming thought, let's remember that God
too, has his 'secret weapon', and that weapon is, quite
simply, love. God's been picking out his targets right down
the centuries, and, when he turns his secret weapon of love
on them, he just shrivels up all the hate and anger in their
hearts.

Take Paul, for instance. Before he became a Christian, he
was on the other side, trying hard to arrest Christians and
frighten them into giving up their religion. But God aimed
his love at Paul, and just burnt away all the hatred that Paul
felt. So Paul turned right round and became a Christian himself, one of the greatest there has ever been.

Or, to come to our own times, take a man called Fred.

He'd been a criminal for many years, who'd burgled houses and stolen people's money and goods. Not only that, he was violent and had beaten people up and hurt them. Finally, he was caught and put in prison, out on Dartmoor. There he stayed in his prison cell, a grim and dangerous character, his heart full of hate. But then God turned his secret weapon on Fred. Fred heard the story of Jesus and began to think more and more about him. Finally something wonderful happened: God won his battle and Fred became a Christian. All the old bitterness was destroyed by the power of God's love. Now Fred is out of prison and is a new man: he runs a shop during the week and preaches in church on Sundays.

God's weapon of love can reach the most unlikely targets.

Romans 5: 6–8

Loving God,
You know all about us,
the bad and hateful things inside us which fight against you,
as well as the good and lovely things.
Win your victory of love in our lives,
so that we may be on your side,
now and evermore.

OUT OF THE DEEP

It was a cold April night in the North Atlantic as the great ship — the largest liner ever built — surged forwards through the darkness. The temperature outside did nothing to lessen the gaiety aboard this great floating hotel, ablaze with electric light. The band played in the ballroom, and couples in evening dress strolled along the vast expanse of the deck. But, suddenly, a sickening judder ran through the length of the ship, which at once began to lose speed. The liner, which was called the '*Titanic*' had hit an underwater iceberg and had torn a great rent in its side, far below the waterline. The great vessel was doomed, although it took three hours more before it finally sank. The date was 14th April, 1912.

You can imagine how it must have felt to have been one of the passengers during that terrible time. As soon as it was realised what had happened, the alarm bells rang, and they were all told to gather on deck. With fumbling fingers they put on their life-jackets and waited for their places in the ship's boats. But they soon found out there weren't enough boats for everybody. Naturally some people were panic-stricken when they saw how things were.

The ship's band went on playing to the last, to take everyone's mind off the disaster: but when at the end the deck began to tilt steeply, and it was clear that the liner was going down any minute, they played one last tune. It was the hymn —

> 'Nearer, my God, to thee,
>   Nearer to thee!
> E'en though it be a cross
>   That raiseth me:
> Still all my song shall be,
> Nearer, my God, to thee,
>   Nearer to thee!'

When the '*Titanic*' sank 711 people were saved; but over 1,300 others died. Perhaps some at least in their last moments found strength and hope when they heard that hymn being played.

When things get bad, all sorts of people turn to God, and discover that he's there to be found. But we haven't got to wait till disaster strikes to make that discovery. It's just the same when everything's going well — we can find help and hope and encouragement if we really want to be 'Nearer, my God, to thee'.

Romans 8: 38–39

Loving Father,
Help us to remember that you are always there,
and that we can never go beyond your reach.
You are with us in this life,
and we can be with you still when this life ends.
Help us to turn to you
in the good times as well as in the bad.

A MATTER OF LIFE AND DEATH

It would kill you if you had too much of it, or if you had too little of it. You can see right through it, but it's quite heavy. We use lots of it each day, but it hardly costs us a penny. At a certain temperature it simply vanishes. What is it?

No doubt you've guessed the answer: it's water! We use it so frequently to drink, to wash, to swim in, that we tend to take it very much for granted. But in many parts of the world it's not like that at all; in fact a considerable part of each day may be spent in the hard and heavy work of getting enough water for the family to survive.

If you were growing up in certain parts of Africa, or India, or the Middle East, for example, there would probably be no fresh, clean water piped to your home, ready for you to use simply by turning on the tap. Instead you might have to walk several miles every day to the nearest well, carrying an old petrol can or a plastic container. Then you would have to take your turn queueing up to get to the well, which might very likely be muddy and fly-infested. After that, you might have to walk for a couple of hours in the midday sun, carrying home the heavy water pot on your head.

But these are the lucky people, because they can at least get water. What would it be like to live in an area like Ethiopia or Chad where, for years at a time, there is simply no rain, so that the wells dry up, the crops won't grow, and the cattle begin to die?

The supply of water is a life and death matter. It must be very satisfying to be someone like Bill, a civil engineer from Southampton, who works for a missionary organisation in Africa. His work is to deal with the problems of too much and too little water, because sometimes he's building good strong road bridges over rivers, so that the road is not washed away when the floods come; at other times he's drilling wells out in remote little villages, where previously people have had to walk a long way for their water.

Next time you drink a glass of water, just remember how fortunate we are to be able to get it from a tap. We need water daily to refresh us and keep our bodies going. But we also have deeper needs, too, than the needs of our bodies. We need to be loved, and encouraged, and sometimes forgiven. Jesus once said he could provide the deep-down refreshment required to meet these needs too, just like a spring of water inside us.

John 4: 7–14

Dear Father God,
We thank you for your precious gift of water.
May we not waste it,
or take it for granted.
Help all those for whom getting enough water
is a daily worry and a daily task.

HOW CLEAN ARE YOU?

When were you last told to go and wash? Probably, if we're honest, we'd admit it happens several times a week. Mothers are worst about this: they're always on at you, asking if your hands are clean for lunch, or boring on about that ink stain on your arm, or nagging about the odd speck of dirt behind the ears. That's mums all over.

Yet they have got a point. If we take a look down a microscope at the water we have just washed in, probably we'll get a shock: we'll see bugs hopping about all over the place.

Even if we're the cleanest person that ever lived, we still won't be clean enough for every situation. Take an operating theatre in a hospital, for instance. We've all seen what it's like on television, and we know that anybody who goes in must be scrubbed and clean, and covered all over in a sterilised white gown.

Just suppose you were suddenly asked to come in and watch an operation. Well, you might get goosepimples all over and feel too squeamish. But, even if you're planning to be a doctor or a nurse, and would just love the experience, you still wouldn't be allowed in just as you are. Your skin, your clothing, everything on you would not be clean enough, and might cause infection. You'd have to be washed and covered up with a clean garment first.

It's just the same when we think about being clean inside. Most of us are good enough, clean enough within, for most situations. But just imagine you were suddenly called to meet God. If we were honest, we wouldn't feel good enough to meet him, because we'd think about all the times we'd been really mean and unkind, or hadn't quite told the truth, and we'd realise that God knew all about these black spots. To come to God, we'd need somebody good enough to help us and make it possible for us, grubby and grimy as we are, to be accepted by him.

And, of course, that's just what Jesus does. He wraps his goodness round us like a gown, and covers up all that's not very nice within us. We just wouldn't be fit for God's presence otherwise: the Bible tells us that the goodness we can manage ourselves is no better than filthy clothing. But Jesus can cope with all that. He's made it possible for us, whenever we pray, to come close to God, without feeling ashamed any more.

Isaiah 64: 5–6
Hebrews 10: 19–22

Father,
We look at your son Jesus,
and we know his life was dazzling white.
We look at our own lives
and we know that they are a bit shabby and dirty by comparison.
Thank you, that through his goodness

we in our grubbiness
can pray to you in your purity,
and know that we're in your presence.

PROVE IT!

Have you got the sort of friend who from time to time tells
you some rather tall stories? 'Last holidays my dad took me
up into his private aeroplane', 'Over the weekend I climbed
a mountain 5,000 feet high, all by myself', and a whole lot
more just like that?

If so, you probably question whether these exciting
things actually happened. 'Prove it!', you demand, and only
when you've been given some satisfactory evidence are you
prepared to believe it.

Actually, of course, there aren't all that many things that
can be proved — well, really proved, like $2 \times 2 = 4$. There
was once a Frenchman called Descartes who sat down to
make a list of all the things about which he could be absolutely certain. At the end of the day there was really only one
fact about which he felt really sure — the fact that he himself
existed. 'I think', he said, 'therefore I exist'. Only that was
really proved: everthing else was not proved, just more or
less likely to be true.

In fact, we can't go through life proving everything, like
we can in a series of experiments in the chemistry lab. What
we actually do is to learn which people we can trust and
which we can't, from the evidence of the way they behave. If
someone proves to be trustworthy in our experience, then
we're prepared to put our faith in that person. One of the
most important things we have to learn in life is how to know

whom we can trust and whom we can't.

Christians claim that having faith in Jesus is a bit like that. We look at all the evidence — the things he did and said, the sort of person he was, what he does today for people who believe in him: and, on the strength of that, we may decide to put our faith in him and trust him. But we can never actually prove that he's there and that what he said was true. We can only trust him on the evidence.

Do you remember Thomas, who wouldn't believe the other disciples when they said that Jesus had risen from the dead? 'I shan't believe it,' he said, 'unless I can prove it by touching Jesus and putting my fingers in his wounds.' Jesus came and gave him the proof he wanted; but then went on to say how much better it was to have faith in him as a person rather than just to have proof about him.

We can all put our faith in Jesus, even though we can't see him, and we shall discover him to be the most trustworthy friend we will ever meet.

John 20: 24–29

Lord Jesus,
it's so hard for us
to believe in you,
when everyone around us
wants watertight proof.
Help us to see your goodness and truth and love,
and to put our trust in you, as a person,
as our Lord and our God.

LAUNCHING OUT

Why is it that people love to fly? Some businessmen, of course, spend much of their time jetting round the world, though airliners can be noisy and boring if you are in them for long periods. For sheer enjoyment, it's a much greater thrill to float gently across the sky with no sound at all, and with plenty of time to gaze at the beautiful countryside spread out far below. And that's why every summer thousands of people take to the air in gliders, while others even float away beneath enormous hot-air balloons.

There's a particular spot in the South of England where you can climb to the top of some smooth, grassy Downs, and watch gliders being launched. It's quite high up there, and you get a lovely view across the Sussex countryside stretching away beneath you into the distance.

The launching is done like this. The pilot straps himself into the cockpit of his lightweight craft. Two friends take a firm grip on the tailplane of the glider, which rests on the grass, perhaps fifty yards from the edge overlooking a sheer drop of some hundreds of feet. The middle of a long elastic rope fits into a hook on the underside of the plane's body and stretches forwards in a wide 'V' shape. Two men grab this rope, one on each end, and begin to walk towards the edge of the grassy cliff. As the rope stretches, so their task becomes harder. At last they reach the brink, with the rope stretching tightly back to the glider, which sits like a stone in a catapult sling. When all is ready, the pilot gives a signal, his other friends release the tail, and at once the glider shoots forward towards the drop. Just when you think it's going to topple over the edge and crash, it rises gently from the ground and takes flight, dropping its launching rope and floating out smoothly into space.

Now all this looks very alarming to the spectator, but of course it's all been carefully worked out and is really very safe. Nevertheless, it must give you a funny feeling in your stomach, when you take your glider up in this way for the first time. With your head you know it makes sense; you've watched other people do it with ease, and you trust them; nevertheless actually doing it yourself requires a courageous step of faith.

Of course, we often have to take similar steps of faith, moving forward in the direction we think we should go. You may know someone quite well, but perhaps a time comes when you must decide whether to trust him with a secret. Or you may have to trust your swimming instructor who tells you to take your first dive into the pool. We're always taking little steps like that, first using our minds and then trusting in faith.

Believing in Jesus is really very similar; even though we can't see him, we know a lot about him, both from the Bible, and perhaps from friends who already trust in him. If we make up our minds that he's trustworthy, then we also may want to launch out in faith and trust him too. If we do, he doesn't let us down.

John 20: 24–29

Lord Jesus,
show us how to use our minds.
Show us whom we may trust.
Help us to put our faith in you,
so that in you we may find a friend
who will never let us down.

ROYAL CHILDREN

What do you like doing when you're on holiday? Do you head for the beaches, and spend all your time lying on the sand or poking about for crabs? Or do you like fun-fairs and zoos? Or do you occasionally enjoy visiting famous places and wonderful buildings?

If you've ever had a holiday near London, you've probably been to see Windsor Castle. It's a splendid place, with its walls and turrets that you can see from miles away, and the vast green expanse of the Great Park beside it. The guardsmen in scarlet look magnificent up against the grey stone, and once you're inside there's lot to see, from the Royal Dolls' House to the view from the battlements.

Sometimes when you go there, you'll see the royal standard glinting in gold as it flies from the great flag-pole on the Round Tower. When you see that, you know that the Queen herself is in residence. For Windsor isn't just a great castle; it's also a family home. Ever since William the Conqueror built it 900 years ago, it has been lived in by the royal family, and has been home for them.

What an exciting place in which to grow up! They say that every Englishman's home is his castle, but how about having a castle for a home? It must be a great place for 'Hide and Seek', and if you get tired of playing indoors, then there are miles and miles of parkland to explore.

There is a story told about the Queen when she was a little girl and just a princess, and her father, King George, was on the throne. With her sister, Princess Margaret, she had gone on a long walk to the far side of the park, and had got well and truly lost. Finally, the two little girls knocked on the door of a cottage, and asked the old lady who lived there how they could find their way back to the castle. The old lady told them, and then, suspecting who they were, asked the little girls their names.

'I'm nobody,' said the princess, 'but my father's the King.'

Now that's something that anyone who's a Christian can say. We may not feel we are terribly important, or very clever or gifted. But we matter nevertheless, because Jesus has told us we can be his brothers and sisters, and that makes us children of the same heavenly King.

1 *John* 5: 1–2

Heavenly Father,
We thank you that you care for each one of us,
and that we're all members of your family.
Help us to remember that we matter
because Jesus has called us to be
his brothers and sisters.

WHERE GOD LIVES

There was once a girl called Debbie, who'd reached the age of seven without ever having gone inside a church in her life. So one day her mum decided that she's take her inside one and show her what it was like.

She collected Debbie after school and told her that she'd got a special treat in store for her. Then they set off to the local parish church, which was called St Matthew's. It was a cold afternoon in November with a touch of rain. By the time they reached the church, it was already beginning to get dark.

They found the church door and, to their relief, it was unlocked. It opened with a creak and let them into a vast and gloomy building. Inside it was even more chilly and damp than it had been outside. St Matthew's wasn't very clean, and, even in the gloom — for there were no lights — Debbie could see one or two cobwebs.

Slowly they walked across to the great space in the middle, their feet tapping loudly on the stone floor. Then they stopped and looked around them.

Debbie — who was secretly a bit disappointed, if this was supposed to be a treat — gazed up at the dark roof in silence; then she tugged her mum's sleeve, and said, rather loudly, 'Mum!'.

'Shhh, dear,' said her mother, (because a lot of people think children shouldn't talk in church.)

But Debbie wasn't going to be shushed, 'Mum, who lives here?'

'It's God's house,' answered her mum. 'God lives here.'

Debbie thought about that for a moment, and looked round at the cold, dark, dusty old building. Then she said thoughtfully — 'Mum, if I was God, I'd move!'.

Now, of course, Debbie had got it a bit wrong, because God doesn't actually live in any Church building. But she was right in a way, because he does live in the real Church, made up of all the people who believe in him. Perhaps he has even thought at times of moving out, and leaving us when his people have been particularly disobedient or unkind.

But somehow he's never done it, and he is still found among his people wherever they gather for worship, or wherever people really love him and try to serve him the best way they can.

Even if sometimes we fail to live as he wishes, he never gives up on us, his Church, any more than our parents give up on us, if at times we're naughty and disobedient. They go on loving us underneath, and so does God.

Hebrews 13: 1, 5–6

Dear Father God,
we know you must get very fed up with us,
when we are unkind,
or tell lies,
or are bad-tempered,
and yet you don't give us up.
So please help us to love you back
a little better everyday.

TRYING AGAIN

Have you ever had a friend who has let you down badly? Perhaps said things about you which weren't true, or promised to do something for you and never did it? Or maybe didn't stick up for you, as a friend should, when someone else was being unkind about you?

If you've ever been let down like that, then you'll begin to understand how Jesus felt about Peter. Do you remember that when Jesus was arrested by night and taken for trial, Peter let him down then by pretending he wasn't really a friend of Jesus. Peter was so ashamed of himself on that occasion that he burst into tears and promised to do better.

But there's also a story that, much later on, after Jesus had died on the cross, and then risen from the grave, and finally had gone back to be with God, Peter let him down once again. It happened in the following way. By then, Peter had left Jerusalem and gone to be a leader of the Church in Rome, the very centre of the Roman Empire. But the time came when the Roman Emperor decided to punish the Christians, though they hadn't done anything wrong. So he had them hunted down, beaten, tortured, and even killed. Now when this began to happen, Peter became scared and decided to run away, even though he was the leader of the Christians, before he too was caught and killed. As he was leaving Rome hurriedly in the middle of the night, suddenly, just outside the city, he had a vision of Jesus coming towards him.

Jesus stopped him on the road and said quietly, 'Peter, where are you going?'

'I'm leaving, Lord,' said Peter, 'Before they catch me and kill me — crucify me, perhaps.'

'In that case,' said Jesus, 'I must go into the city and be crucified all over again for you.'

At this Peter was so ashamed that he turned round and went back to Rome, where he was indeed arrested and crucified for his faith. This time, he hadn't let Jesus down.

Matthew 26: 69–75

Lord Jesus,
We let you down so often,
by what we do or by what we say,
or by being scared to do what's right.
Help us to remember Peter
and to know that you will help us too
to try again,
and to do better next time.

GOING FOR A GOLD

If you could represent your country in the Olympic Games, what sport would you take up? Do you fancy yourself as a long distance runner? Or how about the high jump, or throwing the discus? Or what about streaking down the swimming pool in pursuit of a record time? Can't you just imagine how you'd feel, standing up there on the platform after you'd won, with all the television cameras whirring and with the National Anthem playing? What an unforgettable moment!

One thing's for certain: if you really want to reach the Olympic standard in your favourite sport, then the time to start training is now. Athletes aren't made in a day. They're produced by long, hard years of tough training.

The same is true of doing anything worthwhile. If you're serious about it, then you've got to give it everything you have. It will mean giving up a lot to train really well. If you want to be a surgeon when you grow up, then you'll need to spend years learning all about the human body and its diseases. And if you want to be an architect or an engineer, you've got to be prepared to study for a really long time, in just the same way.

It's similar when it comes to being a Christian. Paul, one of the greatest Christians of all time, speaks as though he was talking about training to win a race. He thought that doing God's work was so worthwhile that he didn't mind if it sometimes made life very hard for him. He encountered many people who hated him for what he was doing, and he was stoned, beaten, and shipwrecked in the course of his adventurous life. Yet he thought it was all worthwhile, because for him nothing was more important than doing what he believed God was telling him to do.

Philippians 3: 12–14

Dear Father God,
Thank you for athletes and sportsmen,
who train hard to do well.
Teach us to give our very best
to whatever we are doing
for in that way we serve you.

GETTING WHAT YOU ASK FOR

Have you ever asked mum and dad for something you really wanted, only to find that they said 'no', however much you begged and pleaded? It seems so obvious that you know what things you really need, yet unaccountably your parents seem to think they know better. How can they be so blind?

Perhaps you feel you really must buy some fireworks for Guy Fawkes Day, or the Fourth of July, and you ask dad for some money to get them with.

'No,' he says, 'I'm not letting you buy your own fireworks: but I will take you down to the firework party that is being organised and run by the town council.'

So you go along, a bit grudging about it, only to find that it is actually a much better show than you could ever have managed by yourself, with colossal rockets, and enormous bangers.

The fact is that mum and dad actually do know better than you what you really need — which may not be the same thing as what you think you want.

It's a bit like that with God. We're always asking him for lots of things in our prayers. Sometimes we are given what we ask for; but sometimes God gives us something even better.

A man once wrote down his thoughts about how God treats our prayers. He was an American, a soldier in the Civil War (1861–65), and what he wrote was found in his pocket after his death —

> I asked God for strength, that I might achieve;
> I was made weak, that I might learn humbly to obey.
> I asked for health, that I might do greater things;
> I was given infirmity, that I might do better things.
> I asked for riches, that I might be happy;
> I was given poverty, that I might be wise.
> I asked for power, that I might have the praise of men;
> I was given weakness, that I might feel the need of God.
> I asked for all things, that I might enjoy life;
> I was given life, that I might enjoy all things.
> I got nothing that I asked for — but everything I had hoped for.
> Almost despite myself, my unspoken prayers were answered.
> I am, among all men, most richly blessed.

Matthew 7: 9–11

Loving Father,
Help us always to remember
that you know us better than we know ourselves,
and love us better than we love ourselves.
When we ask you in our prayers for what we want,
help us to trust you to give us what we need.

LOST AND FOUND

Just suppose you are away on holiday by the sea, and you decide to go down to the beach for a swim. When you get there, you see remarkable sight: a group of seven or eight people walking round and round in a circle on the soft sand, kicking it up as they go. Amongst them is a hot and angry young man. And sitting on the ground nearby, crying her eyes out, is a very bedraggled young lady. Now what on earth do you think is going on?

Well, somebody actually saw this scene on a beach. What had happened was this: the young man and the girl had only been married for a few days, and were, in fact, away on their honeymoon. Unfortunately, the wedding ring didn't fit too well on the young lady's finger and, as she got ready to swim, the ring fell off into the sand. The young man was angry because he thought she'd been careless. And the holiday-makers sitting around had been so sorry for the couple that they had all joined in the search, actually making things far more difficult by churning up the sand with their feet.

However, the story has a happy ending, because somehow or other, the ring was found, and everybody was very pleased about it. A wedding-ring is far too precious to lose without having a really good search for it.

Jesus told a story about a housewife who lost a valuable coin, and practically turned the house upside down in her efforts to find it. He was telling us that, just as there are some things so precious that we'll move heaven and earth to find them if they get lost, so, even more, God cares for each one of us and will do everything he can to find us if we are lost.

Luke 15: 8–10

Jesus,
Thank you for the story of the lost coin;
help us to see just how precious
each one of us is to the Father,
who doesn't want any of us to get lost.

WHAT DO YOU WANT?

What do you do when you have decided there is something you absolutely must have? Suppose there is some particular toy in the toyshop — a radio-controlled model car or a talking doll which you've had your eyes on for weeks: you'll do everything you possibly can to buy it. You'll save up your pocket-money, do some jobs for the neighbours to earn a little more, touch dad for a loan, or wheedle gifts out of visiting aunties. One way and other you'll scrape together the money you need, and eventually the day will come when you can go to the shop and buy that thing you've been treasuring in your mind for so long.

There was once a man, who, just like you, wanted something very much. What he wanted, though, wasn't an object in a shop window, but a spot where he could build the house of his dreams. As a young student from Sweden, he'd visited the island of Capri, just off the coast of Italy near Naples. It's a beautiful place, with lush green trees against the vast cliffs of grey granite in the background. There are little flat-roofed white houses, surrounded by sweetly-scented flowers, and amongst them the ruins of old Roman buildings.

The student fell in love with this beautiful island, where, in those days, few people lived. One spot particularly caught his fancy — a flat shelf of rock up towards the highest point on the island, with a breathtaking view over the Bay of Naples. It seemed 'to him just the very site for his house especially as it already had on it the ruins of a Roman villa.

But what could he do about it? He was only a student, training to be a doctor, and, of course, he had no money. However, he worked hard at his studies, qualified, and started his work in Paris. He became a very good doctor, who was able to help and to heal many people. Before long he had enough cash saved up to go back and buy that lovely plot on Capri, though it took him many more years before he had all the money he needed to build the house of which he'd dreamed for so long.

The man's name was Axel Munthe, and you can see his dream house if you visit the island of Capri, although he died in 1949. He had loved Italy and its people, and had shown his gratitude for the beauty of Capri by giving his services as a doctor in Naples, when the terrible disease of cholera had come to that city, bringing many deaths. He'd really wanted to build that house, in its lovely situation, and to do it he'd been prepared to work hard for many years.

Jesus told a story about a man who wanted something very much indeed, and was willing to sell everything he had to buy it. When Jesus told this story, what he was saying to us was this: the thing that's really worth having above everything else is the Kingdom of God — that means, living your life the way God wants you to. It's worth giving up everything, to do that, for the Kingdom of God is the most precious thing you could ever imagine — better than that toy in the shop window, better even than a dream-house on Capri.

Lord God,
Help us to know
that serving you
is the really important thing,
and help us to want to do this
above everything else.

WHAT'S REALLY IMPORTANT?

If you were given just five minutes to get ready to leave your
home for ever, what would you do? Would you run about
collecting at least a few of your most precious things to take
with you — perhaps a tape-recorder or a camera or your
stamp-collection. Or would you look for your pets to scoop
them up, to make sure they came away safely? Or would you
help mum and dad get ready, or make sure gran was alright
and knew she had to leave?

Difficult decisions like these must once have faced the
people living in a little Italian town. It was a morning in
August, hot and oppressive, and on that day there was a
curious stillness in the air, as people went about their normal
tasks and, when it reached midday, began to get ready for
lunch.

Suddenly there was a most tremendous explosion, causing
the whole town to shudder with the shock of it. Immediately people ran out into the streets, gazing anxiously up
towards the great mountain which loomed over the town;
for the name of the town was Pompeii, the year was AD 79,
and the mountain was the volcano Vesuvius.

The eruption that followed must have been terrible. In that first shattering thunderclap the whole summit of the mountain had dissolved into red hot debris and molten lava, and had been blown skywards: now all this began to rain down upon the surrounding countryside. Soon the people of Pompeii found they were being bombarded with stones and burning ash, and the air became thick with foul gases. They realised that they must leave at once if they were to escape with their lives.

And so they fled as fast as they could, away from that terrible mountain, which was still belching out destruction. Most of them left all their possessions behind, but got away to safety themselves. Some, however, were so bothered about their money and all their works of art that they stayed to try to save them, and in so doing were overcome by the fumes and died.

When things go badly wrong, it makes us think what really matters most to us. People are so much more precious than our possessions, and what we are is so much important than what we have. And this is precisely what Jesus was always trying to teach us, telling us in many different ways that it's vital for us to think first about God rather than about money, and to serve him by looking after one another.

Luke 12: 16–21

Lord Jesus,
Help us to see what really matters.
Help us to love and serve you first of all,
and to show our love
by caring for those around us.
Help us to put people before things,
and to care about others more than about money,

remembering that you cared about us so much
that you gave your life for us.

THINKING TALL

Have you ever had the great annoyance of finishing some
complicated piece of work, only to realise that it won't do
after all, and that you've got to go right back to the beginning and start all over again? Perhaps you've worked out
some difficult mathematical calculation, and then discovered
that your answer is wrong.

That could mean you've wasted twenty minutes work.
That's bad enough, but how about discovering you've
wasted not twenty minutes but thirty-one years of back-
breaking toil? It would put anybody off from starting again.

Yet that's precisely what the builders of Salisbury
Cathedral had to do. The first Cathedral stood outside the
present city of Salisbury, up on a little hill called today Old
Sarum. It was there that the Normans built the first
Cathedral, not long after William the Conqueror landed in
1066. It took them, in all, thirty-one years to complete the
building.

But the clergy of the Cathedral had to share their windy
hill-top with the soldiers who manned the castle next to the
great church, and, as time went on, it became obvious that,
up on that plateau, there wasn't enough water to drink or
space for everybody to live together. There were fearful rows
between soldiers and clergy: one night the guards locked out
all the clergymen, and wouldn't allow them back up onto
the defended hill-top! Eventually it became clear to the
clergy that the only answer was to leave the fine church that

had taken so long to build, and to start all over again somewhere else.

So they moved to an open site down by the river. This time the building work took thirty-eight years, but the results were splendid. When they'd gone on to add a magnificent spire — the tallest in England — everybody agreed that the final result was beautiful and that the move had been worth all the effort. So Salisbury Cathedral stands today like a great pencil pointing up into the sky, glorifying God by its beauty and reminding everyone who visits it that God is above everything we do.

Only the best we can give is good enough for God. That's why those early builders toiled away so hard and so long. But we don't have to build cathedrals to praise God: we can do it just by the way we tackle our own tasks. If we give our very best in what we do, then that's good enough for him.

1 *Corinthians* 15: 58

Dear Lord God,
as we wonder at the beauty of great cathedrals,
help us to honour those who made them to your glory,
and encourage us by their example.
You know what we are and what we can do.
You know when we are not really trying,
and when we are doing our very best.
Help us to praise you just by the the way we do our work —
making it the best thing we can give.

USING OUR GIFTS

Oxford is an important city, and its great university is a famous place of learning. Over the centuries it has produced authors and thinkers, politicians and playwrights, scholars and saints. It is also a very beautiful place, with many fine buildings and bridges.

In a rose garden, just next to a lovely old bridge over the River Cherwell, there is a little stone slab, in memory of a scientist who made one of the most valuable discoveries of this century. His name was Sir Alexander Fleming, and it was in 1928 that he discovered the substance that he came to call 'penicillin'. Together with two other scientists, Florey and Chain, he went on to develop this new discovery which, with its amazing capacity to kill germs, has since then saved millions of people's lives worldwide. Fleming, with his two friends, received the Nobel prize for medicine in 1945.

Fleming was a man who'd been given brains and intelligence, and he had to work hard and carefully to carry out his work. Just suppose that he'd done nothing about his wonderful discovery, but had just filed his notes under 'P' in his filing cabinet: what a terrible waste that would have been.

But instead he used his gifts to the full, making the very most out of what he'd been given. The result was a great blessing for mankind.

We've all been given a gift of some kind, even if we're not sure yet what it is. That gift is for us to use and make the most of in helping others. That's the best way we have of saying 'thank-you' to God for what he's given us.

Luke 19: 11–27

Father,
We thank you for all that you've given us,
for our brains and our bodies,
our skills and our talents.
Help us to remember that you trust us
to use all we have to the full,
in the service of others,
and in praise of you.

OFFERING UP

What are you like at practical do-it-yourself jobs at home? Do you help dad when he is mending things, fetching the hammer and nails, or holding the ladder for him? Or perhaps you're more skilful than that, and can put up a couple of shelves on the wall all by yourself. If so, you'll know just how satisfying it is when you can look at a job well done, and see joints that really do come together properly, and nails that are driven in straight and true.

Proper carpenters have got an expression they use when they are half way through making something, and they hold together the bits they've made so far to see if they fit properly: they call this — 'offering it up'.

Some of the finest craftmanship in England is to be seen in the beauty of medieval Cathedrals. Take Salisbury, for instance. Its spire — at 404 feet — is the tallest in the country. On each side of it are decorative carvings called 'ball flowers': these are little round human heads, and there must be hundreds of them on that spire. You can't see the detail from below, but you can be sure that those at the top are carved just as skilfully as those at the bottom. The craftsmen who made them could also be said to have 'offered them up', giving them to God as their own personal gift.

And so it can be with us. Anything we make really well can be turned into a present for God, just by our remembering to thank him for giving us the materials and the skills. In this way, we'll be offering up our work in gratitude to God.

1 *Chronicles* 29: 11–14

Dear God,
the maker of all things,
the great craftsman,
we thank you for this wonderful world,
and for the skills you give to men.
Thank you for letting us make things,
which give us joy in the making.
Help us to offer up our work to you
in praise and gratitude.

2

TIMES TO REFLECT

LIFE IN THE FAMILY

What family occasions do you like most? In most families there are lots of special times when we make sure we're all together to enjoy them — family weddings and parties, Christmas and Easter, holidays together, Sunday lunch. You'd be a poor member of your family if you never showed up when everyone else in the family was there, enjoying each other's company.

It's a bit like that with God's special family, the Church. The Church is really people, not a building. It's all of us when we gather for school assembly, or attend Sunday School, or take part in a Sunday service. We're meant not just to go to the church building, but to be members of the Church family. God wants us all to be there on the special occasions, like the services on Sunday, so that we can worship him, and meet one another. Only in this way can we really do our bit to help and have all the fun of being a real member.

There was once a minister up in the Highlands of Scotland, who looked after a small congregation of country people at his little church. He began to notice that one member of the church, a shepherd, was coming to the church much less regularly than he used to.

One afternoon he went up to visit him at the whitewashed cottage on the hillside where he lived. The shepherd received him gravely and showed him to a seat at the fireside. In silence they sat and stared at the glowing red fire in the grate. Then the minister picked up the tongs and lifted a hot coal out of the fire and on to the hearth. They watched it without a word as it gradually cooled down and slowly grew grey and cold. Then the minister got up and went home.

The next Sunday the shepherd was back in his usual seat in the church. He'd got the message: by staying away from the warmth of the Church family the shepherd was letting something in his own heart grow cold.

John 15: 1–4

Father,
We thank you that we can belong
both to our own family at home
and also to your special family, the Church.
Help us to be good members of both,
being there, doing our share,
and enjoying the fun of belonging.

PARTY TIME

What happens when you have a party? No doubt you ask all your friends along, and mum makes lemonade and jellies and a great big cake. Probably you have some games, and almost certainly there will be presents. And quite likely you have a big bunch of balloons tied on to the front gate, just to let everyone know it's happening, and that everybody's enjoying themselves.

Have you ever thought that going to church should be a bit like that? After all, on Christmas Day, we go to give thanks for Jesus' birthday, and every Sunday's meant to be a chance for the friends of Jesus to get together with him, and to celebrate.

There's a church in Washington D.C. where they organise the Sunday services just like a special weekly party. Everyone's pleased to see their friends there, so there's quite some time given over to welcoming and greeting. The clergyman's chair has got lots of balloons tied to it, just to show it's a celebration. And, when the service is over, everybody stays on for a cup of coffee, or to have lunch together.

Perhaps it's not always quite like that at your church, or maybe only at Christmas time; but nevertheless, Christians are always happy to come together to worship. After all, if Jesus himself is there, then there really is something to celebrate, isn't there?

Colossians 3: 14–17

Jesus,
You've promised that,
whenever your friends gather together,
you'll be there with them.
Help us to see
that church is really a party
and every Sunday a celebration.

GETTING READY

Do you like having guests to stay? Part of the fun at Christmas time is to have a chance to meet other members of the family, perhaps having your granny, or a favourite uncle and aunt for a few nights. Family get-togethers are, after all, part of what Christmas is all about.

But family get-togethers don't just happen. They have to be organised and prepared for and that means a whole heap of hard work, most of it falling to mum. It's mum who has to think about what everyone will eat, and it's mum who has to clean the rooms and make the beds and cook the meals. After all, it wouldn't be much good if granny turned up and nobody had got her bed ready or made the room look nice for her.

Now it is just like that when we think about not just Christmas family parties, but Christmas itself. After all, the first Christmas day was a great family occasion, when the Son of God came to be with the whole human family. Then, people weren't ready to receive him: there was no room for him at the inn. So nowadays we give everybody a chance to get ready to remember that first Christmas day — four weeks of 'getting ready' time, in fact, which we call 'Advent'.

But, of course, at Christmas time we don't simply remember what happened so long ago at Bethlehem: we do more than that. We can actually invite Jesus now to be the invisible guest in our home, to be welcomed in to share in our lives —

> 'Where meek souls will receive him,
> Still the dear Christ enters in.'

John 1: 10–14

Lord Jesus,
We'd like to think that
you'd feel at home
in our family and in our lives.

But we know there are things to be put straight —
quarrels sorted out and unkind words forgiven —
before it would be right to ask you in.
Help us to get ready properly for your coming,
and then to enjoy you as our welcome guest.

WHAT'S MUM WORTH?

Have you ever asked yourself just how many hours work mum puts in each week in simply looking after you? That means adding up all the time she spends cooking, washing, ironing, and all the other jobs that make up a mother's work.

There was once a boy called Norman who wasn't too concerned about what mum did for him, but got terribly bothered when he thought of all the work he did to help mum — work for which he wasn't paid or properly appreciated. So he thought he ought to remind his mother about all his unrewarded labour, in the hope that she might increase his pocket money in recognition of all his services.

So, one evening, he wrote out a long bill and slipped it under mum's pillow. It went like this:

To Mum, for orl my hard werk this weke —

making my bed (sumtimes)	10p
woshing up (twice)	20p
cleneing my tethe	10p
walking the dog (wunze)	20p
TOTAL	60p
plus VAT	9p
Grand Total	69p

Sined: Norman

After leaving her this message Norman felt quite sure mum would appreciate all his work, and would pay him accordingly. Imagine her surprise when she said nothing at all to him about his note, throughout the day, but just carried on as usual.

Norman felt sure she couldn't yet have found it under her pillow, so he just waited.

Then, at bedtime, when he pulled out his pyjamas, he found a letter under his own pillow. It read like this:

> For looking after Norman, night and day, for ten years; feeding him, keeping him clothed, and loving him at all times, even when he's naughty . . .   £0–0p.

and underneath she had signed it — 'with all my love, Mum', and she'd put some crosses for kisses.

When Norman read this, he went very quiet and he felt rather small. And ever after that he was particularly grateful for everything his mum did for him.

We do take our mothers for granted, and that's why it is good to have Mothering Sunday to remind us of mum's love and care, and to give us a chance to say 'thank you.' For, actually, a mother loves her children in just the same way that God loves us — freely and all the time, even when we don't deserve to be loved, and do things which are hurtful to Him. In this way, mum can teach us what God is like.

1 *John* 4: 7–12

Dear Father God,
we thank you for all mothers,
for the way they love their children,
and care for them in so many ways.
Help us to be grateful for all the care we receive,

and to be thankful that we are always loved,
even when we don't deserve it.

HE LIVES!

If somebody out of the blue said to you the word 'fish', what
is the first thoughts that would come to your mind? Probably, you'd come up with the word 'chips'. Similarly 'ham'
might suggest 'burger', and 'milk' might prompt 'shake'.

But suppose you were given an unusual word, such as
'Easter': what does that make you think of? 'Chicks'?
'Chocolate eggs'? 'Cake'? Probably! But there's a lot more
to Easter than that. It may be a word that sparks off all sorts
of nice ideas to do with what we give each other at East-
ertime, and it may conjure up pictures of spring weather,
lovely flowers, and new life.

Deep down, though, it has an even more exciting mean-
ing, because it's all about Jesus rising from the dead and
showing us that he is still alive. The Bible tells us how some
of the disciples went to his tomb on the third day after his
death on the Cross, only to find the tomb empty and Jesus no
longer there. Then, later, he actually met them, risen from
the dead and fully alive. And he promised his friends that he
would be with them evermore.

That's the real reason why Easter is such a very special day
for Christians — a day of victory and hope. It's such good
news that it spills over from Easter Sunday onto every Sunday, so that each week we're reminded of the message that
Jesus lives.

This was realised by African Christians in Uganda some
years ago. At that time terrible things were being done in

Uganda under the cruel government of President Amin. Eventually, one of the church leaders, Archbishop Janani Luwum dared to stand up to the President, and to resist the lawless way that his police had been arresting and killing people without trial. At once he was arrested himself and a few days later he was shot, though the government pretended that he'd died in a car crash while trying to escape.

All his Church people were very sad, and they planned a great service for his burial on the following Sunday, at the Cathedral in Uganda's capital, Kampala. The grave had been dug and everything prepared, but at the last minute the police refused to hand over his body; they said that the Archbishop had already been buried somewhere else in the country, but actually they didn't want anyone to find out that he had been murdered, and not killed in an accident.

The service went on, nevertheless, and at the end of it, everyone came out of the Cathedral and stood round the empty grave, in sorrow. But as they stood there they realised that this empty grave was actually a sign of hope. They were reminded of what the angel had said to the two women who came to the tomb of Jesus: 'Why do you seek the living among the dead?' Their sorrow was turned into joy, and they began to sing a great hymn of praise.

So, when we hear the word 'Easter' it should remind us, not just of flowers and chicks, but of Jesus coming to be with his friends and to give them life and hope.

Luke 23: 55 to 24: 9

Lord Jesus,
We thank you that your death on the cross
was not the end of the story.
It was sad when you died,

but wonderful when you rose again.
Help us to know that you are there,
invisible but wonderfully alive,
to be with us always.

POWER FOR LIVING

What's the most wonderful of man's discoveries that we use everyday? Computers? Cars? Television? Well, perhaps: but not everyone has their own computer or is able to travel daily in a car, and there are plenty of families that don't choose to have a television set. The right answer is, most probably, electricity. It would be almost impossible, in a developed country, to go for a whole day without making use of the hidden power of electricity.

And, when you think about it, how amazing electricity is. You can't see it, smell it, or hear it: but if you connect up a vacuum cleaner, or a radio set, or a standard lamp, or an electric fire, you can have instant power, sound, light, and heat — all by electricity.

So exciting and dynamic is this power that we even use it as a picture word to describe certain people: we talk, for instance, about somebody being 'electrifying', if we mean that he's full of life and go and energy, fun to be with, the sort of person who gives a lift to all around him.

God's like that, too. Of course, he is anyway the source of all light and power, of everything that is: but when somebody discovers God, really becomes willing to know him better and to serve him more, then God in turn comes to meet him. He does this through his Holy Spirit, the most electrifying person you can imagine, even though you can't see him. Sometimes the results can be as dramatic as when you plug in an electrical appliance and switch on the power.

The Holy Spirit came to all the disciples when they were gathered together after Jesus had died, risen from the dead, and gone back to heaven, on the day called 'Pentecost'; and the result was an amazing burst of spiritual energy in their lives.

And that's been happening through the Church's history ever since. There was once, for instance, a clergyman, who, at the age of thirty-five, was very depressed and down-hearted, because his work didn't seem to be getting any-where. He tried being a college chaplain at Oxford, and he tried working in America, and both experiences had left him discouraged because he didn't seem to be able to get through to people.

Then, one day, he went to a church in London to take part in a service, and, during it, as he afterwards wrote, he felt his heart 'strangely warmed'. God, through his electri-fying Holy Spirit, had come to him in a new way.

The results were amazing. The clergyman, whose name was John Wesley, went on to spend the next fifty-three years of his life travelling all over the British Isles, preaching about the love of God and the power of his Spirit. He preached usually in the open air, and people came by the thousand to hear him, particularly from the big industrial towns. Because all this happened 200 years ago, he had to travel on horse-back, and it is estimated that he covered a quarter-of-a-million miles in this way, to preach 40,000 sermons. The people who responded to his message came to be called 'Methodists', and that is why today churches bear that name.

God's Holy Spirit can electrify people, giving them love, power, and energy to do his work.

Acts 2: 1–4

Holy Spirit of God,
you change people's lives,
when they listen to you,
and you give them fresh power for living.
Guide our lives
so that we may do great things
for you and for those around us.

PARSON HAWKER

Which church festival do you enjoy most? Everybody likes
Christmas, of course, with the carols and the trees ablaze
with lights. But what about Easter time, with all the spring
flowers and the promise of new life? Or Whit Sunday, with
its thrilling message of the gift of the Holy Spirit? Or how
about Harvest Festival in the autumn, with its note of gratitude for all God's goodness?

Even if you only come to church occasionally, you probably come at harvest time, bringing your gifts of fruit,
vegetables, and flowers, which are later to be given away to
old people who are housebound and living on their own.

If you enjoy Harvest Festival, then you have got a very
strange person indeed to thank for it. He was an unusual
clergyman called Parson Hawker, who was Vicar of Mor-
wenstow, a little fishing town on the Cornish coast, during
the first part of the last century.

Parson Hawker enjoyed light and colour, and animals,
and all things growing. He used to wear all sorts of brightly
coloured clothes when he was taking services, and even had

his cat accompany him into the pulpit, to the great surprise of the congregation. He was the first clergyman ever to hold a service of Harvest Festival as we know it. The idea caught on, and before long churches all over England had followed his example.

Parson Hawker did something else during his time in Cornwall, that was both courageous and right. In that period Cornish people were extremely poor, and some of them, to get rich, used to take part in the terrible crime of wrecking. Cornwall has a fierce and rocky coast that can be very dangerous for ships; captains have to keep a close watch on the lighthouses which tell them where danger lies. But evil men used deliberately to shine lights in the wrong places, so that the ships were actually guided onto the rocks. The men would then kill any survivors of the wreck, and steal all the cargo that was washed ashore.

Now wrecking was really both theft and murder, and Parson Hawker hated it for the wicked crime it was. So he spent much of his time preaching, speaking, and writing against the wreckers, despite their threats against him. So successful was he that eventually this terrible crime was stopped altogether.

So, the next time you go to church on Harvest Festival, and see the grapes and the marrows and the chrysan-themums, spare a thought for Parson Hawker, who began it all, and carried on such a brave campaign against those dark deeds on the Cornish coast.

John 15: 16–17

Father,
We thank you for people like Parson Hawker,
who help us to see your goodness in nature,

and who fight bravely against the wicked things
that men do to spoil your world.

FRUITS

What do you do at Harvest Festival time? Do you, for
example, decorate the classroom with bunches of flowers
and baskets of fruit? Or maybe you all go along to the local
church for a special harvest service, and leave your gifts
there. Probably all these lovely things from the garden are
then divided up in to separate parcels and taken out to
elderly and handicapped people shut in at home and unable to
go out. A little present like that can make such a big difference: we all need to know that somebody cares about us.

Of course, having Harvest Festival once a year is really
only a way of saying a big 'Thank you' for the apples and the
oranges, the potatoes and the carrots, the roses and the
daffodils that we enjoy at different times throughout the
year. We enjoy them and we need them. We must eat fruit
and vegetables if we are to grow up with strong, healthy
bodies, and we must have around us the beauty of flowers if
we're really to enjoy God's world.

Even at times when there are no flowers to be had, there
will probably be a large bowl of fruit on the sideboard or on
the kitchen table, brightening up the whole room. That's a
'must' in every home.

And the Bible tells us that there's another kind of fruit,
too, that needs to be around in a family, if life's going to be
really good. These fruits are not to be seen in a basket, but
instead in the lives of each member of the family. For these are
the fruits of the Spirit, that is to say, all the lovely qualities

that God wants to grow inside us if we'll let him. His Spirit
goes round amongst us like an invisible gardener, encourag-
ing love, joy, peace, patience, kindness, goodness, and many
other beautiful things to grow inside each one of us. Without these fruits too our lives and our homes would be sad and
miserable places.

Galatians 5: 22

Dear Father God,
Send us your Holy Spirit,
the silent gardener we cannot see or hear,
and ask him to grow within us
all the lovely fruits of goodness and truth.

MEASURING GROWTH

What's most fun about having a birthday? No doubt your
first thought is getting presents, preferably large and mysterious ones, wrapped up neatly in highly coloured paper.
After that, you might go on to think of parties, preferably
with a large chocolate cake for tea, and a candle for every year
of your life.

But birthdays really are a way of measuring growth, not
simply a reason for having fun, though that comes into it as
well. They are a bit like milestones along a road — there to
help you measure your progress.

In some families they make a great thing of taking the
birthday boy or birthday girl out to that wall in the garage
where everybody's height is marked up in pencil. A little line
is then drawn on the wall to show just how tall you were on

your birthday.

It's quite easy to measure how you are growing up on the outside — how many years you've lived, or how many inches you've grown. What's not so simple is measuring how you are growing up on the inside — how much kinder, more honest, more reliable, and less big-headed you've become over the past year. Wouldn't it be useful if we could find some way of marking that up on the garage wall also!

One thing's certain: if we want to be Christians, then we are meant to grow up in all these important ways. It's a slow process, and hard to measure, but it should be happening none the less. At each birthday, we should be able to look back and see ways in which we've let God help us grow up a bit over the last year! He'll do it, if we ask him.

Ephesians 3:14–19

Dear Father God,
thank you for all the marvellous ways
in which we grow and change —
ways we can see,
and ways which only you can know about.
Help us to be as bothered
about growing up inside,
as we are about putting on another inch
or adding another year.

3

MIRRORS FOR THE LIGHT

ALL SAINTS

The trouble about our new Religious Education teacher is that he's always asking questions. He doesn't just read you great chunks out of the Old Testament, like Miss Spry, the teacher before, used to do. That was OK when she did that; if you liked the story, you could listen with half an ear, and, if you didn't, well, you could always close your eyes and think about your favourite television programme.

Not with Mr Humphries, though: you couldn't sleep in his lessons. For a start, he'd notice right away if you did: but he always makes his stuff just that bit too interesting to let your thoughts wander. It's enough to drive anyone mad.

Here he was, at it again. He'd just told us all about that man Paul, who'd been changed completely after seeing Jesus in a sort of a dream. He didn't read the story, but actually told it to us; you'd think he'd been there himself, right beside Paul.

Now he was throwing questions around the classroom like darts at a dart board. 'Rogers,' he bellowed, 'what are saints?'

Poor old Ginger, he doesn't have much between the ears, and this one had really caught him out. There was a long silence and then suddenly he had an idea. He must have been thinking about the stained glass window down at St Johns, where we sing in the choir together, because he blurted out 'Sir, they're the people the light shines through.'

There was a pause while Mr Humphries considered this. Then he said thoughtfully, 'Rogers, that's really a very good answer. People through whom the light of Jesus shines. And that means all of us who try to be Christians — not just the big names in the Bible, like St Paul, and in the history books. We are all of us supposed to be like that, like windows through which you can see Jesus.'

2 *Corinthians* 4: 5–6

Dear Lord Jesus,
We can read about some great Christians in history,
people through whom your light shines.
Help us to remember
that you want to shine out of our lives too.

ONE OF US

Leprosy is a highly unpleasant disease suffered mainly by people in poorer countries. It is an infections disease which attacks the nerves so that a sufferer gradually finds that he has no feeling left in certain parts of the body — particularly the toes, the fingers, and the face. In this condition, it is very easy to damage yourself — to step on some red hot ash, perhaps, and burn your foot badly without realising it.

Nowadays leprosy can be treated with drugs, and, if caught early enough, checked and cured. But up to a hundred years ago there was no treatment at all that helped, so that down through the centuries people hated and feared lepers, and forced them to live away from everyone else, to prevent the spread of this dreaded disease.

In one area of the Pacific, the authorities selected a deserted island to be a leper colony, where people with leprosy could be left by themselves almost as prisoners, to live out the rest of their lives with only other lepers as company. The island was called Molokai, and the lepers there had no contact with the outside world except just once a month, when a steamer called to leave supplies on the beach, and to land new patients.

One month, however, in the year 1873, the boat came as usual, but this time something very strange happened. Along with the boxes of food there arrived a man who seemed perfectly well, with no sign of the disease. He was a French Roman Catholic priest, and his name was Father Damien. He'd come because he felt deeply sorry for the lepers in their distress and isolation, and he'd made the brave decision to come and join them, to help in any way he could.

For a year he worked among them, nursing the very sick and trying to bring them hope. They were grateful enough, but they couldn't easily accept him, because he wasn't really one of them; he had come of his own free will and could leave again, too, just when he felt like it.

Then one day Father Damien set out to do his washing. He drew some water from the well and put it in a pot to heat up enough to clean his clothes. After a while, he put his finger in the water, to see if it was hot enough, and he discovered something curious: he couldn't feel a thing. He realised that he, too, had caught leprosy.

At once things became very different. The other lepers were sorry for him, and were more ready to receive his help, and to hear what he had to say. Now he was one of them.

Isaiah 53: 2–4

Father, you don't remain far away from this world and its cares,

or turn away from those who need help.
In Jesus, you become one of us
and shared with us the good things and the bad.
Help us to know that,
though we can't see you,
you are always there,
at our side,
ready to help.

SHARING THE SUFFERINGS OF OTHERS

During World War 2, Denmark along with many other countries in Europe, was invaded by the soldiers of Nazi Germany.

At first, life went on much as usual and the invaders behaved correctly. The King of Denmark continued to live in his palace in Copenhagen, and every morning he would ride out of the palace gates on his horse and would tour the city, showing himself to his people to encourage them by his presence among them.

As time went on, the attitude of the enemy invaders changed sharply. Throughout Nazi-occupied Europe a terrible policy had been brought in of rounding up all Jewish people and herding them off to concentration camps. Before the war the German Jews had been persecuted under Hitler. Their rights as citizens had been taken away. Many had fled to other parts of Europe and to the USA. When, in 1940, the German army attacked Denmark the Jews living there knew they were in danger. Soon a poster went up in every town, ordering that, on a certain date, all Jewish people must wear a black armband. This was the first step towards marking the

Jews to single them out and cut them off from their Danish neighbours; the next move would be to arrest them and take them away to almost certain death.

Danish people were horrified at this order, and full of sympathy for the Jews. They waited with dread for the day when the order was to come into force.

When that day dawned, the King rode out of his palace gates as usual, but as he passed the little crowd that always gathered to watch him, there was a gasp of surprise: they saw that he was wearing a black armband.

His example spread like wildfire. Soon so many Danes, who were not themselves Jewish, had joined their Jewish friends in wearing the armband that the order became quite useless: you couldn't tell who were Jews and who were not. So it was that in Denmark at any rate Jewish people were able to survive, thanks to the King's brave action.

Philippians 2: 5–7

Lord Jesus,
Help us to stand beside those who are suffering
because that is what you did
when you gave your life for us on the cross.

THE COST OF CARING

Back in the 1950s Naples was a city with much dirt and poverty. Many people lived in crumbling blocks of flats, separated from their neighbours by narrow little alley-ways hung with washing. Others, even worse-off, crowded into tumbledown huts down on the mud by the sea-shore, in little sheds made of packing cases and other rubbish, with open sewers running amongst them.

Families were large, but parents couldn't afford to look after six or seven hungry youngsters. Boys were normally put out onto the streets to look after themselves when they reached the age of twelve. Not surprisingly, gangs of hungry youths roamed the alleyways, hunting through the garbage and stealing to stay alive.

The city authorities did little to improve matters, but one young priest, Father Borelli, wanted very much to help. However, Borelli knew that the youngsters would never accept somebody wearing a priest's clothes and coming to them from the respectable world of the Church. Fortunately, he had an idea about that, and went off to discuss it with his Bishop.

The next day, one of the gangs found it had a new member, a young man older than the rest, but in jeans and a ragged shirt just like them. For three months Borelli — for that's who it was — lived with the gang, telling nobody who he really was. He shared their way of life, but always managed to keep out of their crimes. His care and willingness to help won many friends.

Then one day he went off in the morning telling the gang to meet him that afternoon in a ruined church they knew. When they came, to their amazement they found their friend dressed as a priest. He explained who he really was and told them that the ruined church could be theirs to live in, if they wished. Because Borelli had become their friend, most of them stayed, and the priest turned the ruin into a real home for the many youngsters who were to come there, to find food, welcome, training and work, and above all, someone who cared for them.

Borelli had succeeded in helping the slum children of

Naples — but only because he was prepared to leave behind his comfort so that he could come alongside them.

Philippians 2: 4–7

Lord Jesus,
You gave up so much
so that you could show us God's love.
Help us to care for others,
even when it's costly to do so.

THE MAN WHO WAS REALLY RICH

There was once a young man who lived in a town in the hills of northern Italy. His father was in the clothing trade and made a lot of money at it. The young man was never short of cash, as his father gave him plenty of pocket money. Like his father, he too enjoyed fine clothing, so he spent a great deal on what he wore, buying only what was the best and the most fashionable. He was a cheerful young man and quite a musician, so he was always being asked out to parties, and had lots of friends.

Somehow, though, there was something missing in his life, and he realised that deep down he wasn't satisfied, despite all the nice things that he had. It wasn't until his town went to war against a city nearby that the young man began to find out what was wrong. Along with all his friends he joined the army, but in his first battle he was taken prisoner, and spent many long months locked up before he was finally set free. During this time he began to see that there was a great deal more to life than just having a good time. He decided he had to do something to help other people, and in this way to serve God.

He began by giving away all his lovely clothes to the poor people and the beggars in his town. This was hard for him to do, and got him into great trouble with his father. But soon he was faced with a much harder test.

As he was riding along one day he met a man suffering from leprosy. Now he was particularly frightened by this terrible disease, and the thought of touching a leper filled him with horror; however, he knew he must do it, if he was really to show him love and sympathy. So he stopped his horse, got down, took the man's hands in his own, and kissed him.

That moment was a turning point in the life of the young man, whose name was Francis. He gathered a group of friends around him, and together they began to live a very simple life, giving away what money they had to help those in need, no longer dressing in fine clothes, but in old brown garments. However, there was plenty of fun in the group, and plenty of music too, because Francis now turned his musical gifts to writing hymns and songs in praise of God.

Francis died nearly 800 years ago, but his friends are still to be seen walking about in their simple brown robes and seeking to help their fellow men. They are called Franciscans, in honour of Francis, the man who discovered the secret of how to become truly rich by giving away all he had.

Matthew 5: 3–10

Lord, make me a channel of your peace.
O Divine Master,
Grant that I may not so much seek —
    — to be comforted, as to comfort

— to be understood, as to understand;
— to be loved, as to love.
For it is in giving that we receive,
it is in forgiving that we are forgiven,
and it is in dying that we are born to Eternal Life.
(from the prayer of St Francis)

GIVING IT AWAY

Suppose you had been given a very large bag of sweets: what would you do with them? Would you hide them away and eat them secretly all by yourself, until you had made yourself sick? Or would you find your special friends and give a few to them, telling them to keep quiet? Or would you make that bag of sweets go as far as possible, by sharing them out amongst anybody who might like to have one?

A problem rather like that faced a man called Henry Smith. Henry was a highly successful jeweller, and, towards the end of his life, he had made a large fortune by his skill and enterprise. Now came the problem: what was he going to do with all the money he'd made? He had neither wife nor children to whom he could leave it, and he felt strongly that he should give it to those in need, particularly poor people living in his own part of England, the county of Surrey.

So he set out to walk round all the parishes in the county, to find out for himself just who the really needy people were. The story is told that sometimes he disguised himself as a beggar and asked for help, just to see how generous the people of a particular parish might be in helping the poor. It is even said that, because of his disguise, he ended up getting into trouble, in some places, and even being put in prison.

Eventually, when he completed his tour, he set about making his will, leaving lots of money to the generous parishes, who clearly knew how to help poor people, but less money, or none at all, to the parishes who had treated him badly, and shown that they didn't care about those in need. There must have been many surprises when his will was opened, and it was discovered how he had shared out his money.

Henry Smith died in 1628, but, through the will that he made, his money is still being given away, just as he directed, to help the poor and the needy.

Jesus told a story once about how we are going to be judged according to the way we have treated other people. It is a reminder to us that everybody matters and is important, even a down-and-out beggar in rags; if every single person is precious in God's eyes then we too must bother about everyone we meet. Whether we say 'yes' or 'no' to helping somebody else really shows whether we are saying 'yes' or 'no' to God himself.

Matthew 25: 31–46

Lord Jesus,
You taught us that
everyone matters to you,
and that there's something of you
in every human being.
So help us to bother about people
and to see them as precious individuals,
just as you did.

OTHERS FIRST

What do you enjoy doing most in winter weather? Do you like skating or sliding on the ice? Or do you prefer snow-balling, or hurtling down a good slope on a toboggan?

An afternoon outside when it's really icy can be great fun: but how about spending endless days and days stumbling through mile after mile of white and silent snow? That, of course, is exactly what the polar explorers have to do. Nowadays they cross the icy wastes of the Arctic and Antarctic on swift motor sledges, but, for the first explorers, progress was very much harder.

One of the most famous of the pioneers was Captain Robert Falcon Scott, of the Royal Navy. He'd been on several Antarctic expeditions, before finally, in the year 1911, he set out to be the first to reach the South Pole.

Dog teams towed their sledges much of the way, but for the last stretch Scott and his four companions left the dogs behind and dragged the heavy sledges themselves. In the end, after a terrible journey which brought them great hardship, they finally reached the South Pole. You can imagine how they felt when they found the Norwegian flag already flying there. They had been beaten to the Pole by just one month, by the Norwegian explorer Amundsen. With heavy hearts, they turned back on the long walk to base.

Quite soon they were in trouble: one member of the small party collapsed and died from cold and strain. The remaining four buried him and toiled on through the snow. They were exhausted, but they still had many miles to stagger to get back to the base where food and supplies waited for them.

It was at this point that one of the four did something that was very courageous and unselfish. His name was Captain Oates, and he was suffering more than any of the others from frostbite. He could get along only very slowly indeed. As they huddled in their little tent one night, Oates realised he could never make it back to base, and that he was only delaying the others. So, making some excuse, he slipped out of the tent into the night, never to be seen again. He gave his life so that the others should have a better chance of surviving. Captain Scott, when he realised what Oates was doing, muttered, 'There goes a very gallant gentleman.'

In the end, none of them made it. They died, after struggling on some way further, just eleven miles from base. Their bodies were eventually discovered, and with them, Scott's diary, from which we learn of the brave and unselfish way in which Captain Oates died, that others might live.

John 15: 12–13

Lord Jesus,
We can see that you gave your life for others,
both by the way you lived,
and by the way you died.
As we think about that fact,
help us to bother more about other people,
and less about ourselves.

ALL I CAN DO

What wakes you up in the morning? Is it the alarm clock? Or the birds singing in the trees? Or perhaps, if you live in the town, it's the clanking of the dustbins as the men come round with the lorry to empty them.

There's one part of the world where it is not the dustcarts that travel the streets in the early morning, but the ambulances. The city of Calcutta in India has a terrible problem of overcrowding and hunger, and hundreds of poor people have to sleep out every night on the streets. Some are ill with disease and lack of food, so every morning the ambulance must go round and collect those who are sick or dying or even dead. It is a very sad thing that there are so many people with nowhere to go, nothing to eat, and nobody to look after them if they're not well.

When a nun from Albania called Teresa visited Calcutta and saw the sick and dying in the streets she decided that something must be done. In 1946 she was given permission. She persuaded the authorities to let her have a disused temple and there she opened a hospital to look after the seriously ill and the dying. Soon the work of Mother Teresa became known, and other nuns of her order came to help her.

Mother Teresa of Calcutta and her friends can only help a few people of course, and there are many thousands in need. Somebody asked her once if it was worthwhile doing what she did, and she gave a very good answer: 'All I can do,' she said, 'is all I can do.' And what she has done is not just to help those in her hospital, but to encourage and inspire people right across the world to do their best for those around them who are in need.

John 6: 5–13

Lord Jesus,
We thank you
for people like Mother Teresa,
and for all the kind and caring people we know.
Help us to learn from their example

and always to try to do our best
for others.

TIME TO SERVE

Have you ever been kept in at school for doing something
wrong? Perhaps somebody was talking during the English
lesson, so the whole class had to stay in during break and do
extra work. It's very hard when you can see all your friends
outside the window happily running around, free to do what
ever they like, while you must stay in.

It is bad enough to be shut in for twenty minutes or half-
an-hour: but how about actually being put in prison, so that
for years on end you are not free to go anywhere and you
have to live your life within a very small area. How terrible
that must be! And yet that's exactly what happened to
thousands of men during World War 2, who were captured
and ended up as prisoners of war.

One such person was a man named John Dodd. He was
serving in the Royal Air Force in Singapore. When the
Japanese invaded, he managed to escape from the doomed
city in one of the last ships to leave, and he landed on the
island of Java. When the Japanese came there too, he managed to hide from them for nearly six months until eventually he was captured. Because he was suspected of being a
spy, he was beaten and tortured for many days before finally
being thrown into a prisoner of war camp. And that's where
he stayed for the next three years, until he was eventually
freed when the war ended.

What would you do after an experience like that? Most of
us would want to have nothing to do with prisons ever

again. But with John, it wasn't like that. Shortly after the war he became a Christian, largely through hearing another former prisoner of the Japanese, Bishop Wilson, speaking about God's love and forgiveness. And the result of his new-found faith was that he felt a great desire to help others who had suffered from the experience of prison.

So John set about his new work, first visiting people in prison, but then going on to set up hostels where people could go after their release, to get used to the outside world once again. Nowadays, there are many of these hostels set up across the country by John Dodd's organisation — the Langley House Trust. There must be hundreds of people who have cause to be thankful for John Dodd's years in prison, and the life to which it led him.

1 *John* 4: 16–21

Dear God,
Thank you for the freedom
to go where we like
and do what we want.
Help us to remember those who are not free
but are shut up in prison.
Remind us that we all need to be forgiven,
and that we all need love, help, and encouragement.

THE VIEW FROM THE SCHOOL GATE

What do you like doing at school during morning break, or after you've finished your lunch, before lessons start again? Do you talk to your friends in the playground? Play cricket or rounders? Or swing on the school gate, watching the world go by outside?

There was once a boy who used to do just that. His school playground had a high railing all round it, and on the other side was a steep road leading up to the parish church and the churchyard nearby. So quite often the boy used to climb up on the gate, or swing on a railing, and watch people passing to and fro on the road.

One day up the road to the church came a small, silent group of people, pushing a hand cart. It was a funeral party, taking a coffin up to the church for the service. The boy watched them with keen attention, for he'd never seen a group like that before. There were only a few mourners and they were obviously very poor indeed; the women wore torn black shawls and the children had bare feet, because their parents couldn't afford shoes for them. Slowly they passed on their way pushing the creaking cart, on which lay the coffin, badly made from a few old planks knocked together.

The sight made a deep impression on the boy. He never forgot it, the memory of this group of poor people was to shape the whole future course of his life. He himself came from a very wealthy family, who lived in a great house in comfort and luxury. It would have been easy to forget all the other people elsewhere, who didn't have enough to eat and who had to work long hours for little pay. It took the sight of those poor people to show the boy just how unfair and unjust the world can be. He decided to do something about it: he would make it his life's work to do what he could for the poor.

The boy's name was Anthony Ashley Cooper, and it was in the year 1816 that he gazed out of the playground at Harrow School at the poor man's funeral. He later became the Earl of Shaftesbury. During his life he worked to pass through Parliament wise and humane laws, cutting down the number of hours that boys had to work in the coal mines, for example, and controlling the way factories were run.

There were many people who had cause to be grateful for the decision he made in his school playground when he was a boy.

1 *John* 4: 19–21

Heavenly Father,
Help us, who have so much,
to remember all those who have so little,
and to learn how to use our lives well
to serve those in need.

LIGHTING A LAMP

Have you ever had to spend time in hospital? Perhaps you've needed to have your appendix out, or maybe you've had trouble with your tonsils. If you've spent some days in a hospital ward, probably you enjoyed the time, and were thoroughly spoilt by all the nurses. No doubt the ward was light and airy, and everything was spotlessly clean.

If that's what you found, then you owe it very largely to a brave lady called Florence Nightingale, who lived a hundred years ago. In those days hospitals were terrible places, dark, dirty, and unhealthy, and there were no well-trained, cheerful nurses to help you.

Florence grew up in a wealthy family and she could have spent her life in comfort, doing very little. Instead, she wanted to help the sick, and so she spent time and effort learning how to do so. In those days nobody thought much of you if you were a nurse, and Florence was considered to be doing something very unladylike. Many people were against her, but she went on studying with great determination.

Then her chance came. Britain was at war with Russia, and many soldiers had been wounded in the fighting. Florence took thirty-seven volunteer nurses and went out to the place where the war was being fought, a part of Russia called the Crimea, on the Black Sea.

The British Generals didn't at all like women coming out to interfere, as they saw it. But they desperately needed good nurses to look after the wounded. So they gave her the army hospital to run. It was in a terrible mess, but Florence and her nurses set to work to clear it up and make it clean. When she went there, on average forty-two out of every hundred wounded men died, because of the dirt and germs and lack of care. With Florence at work, the number dropped to just two out of every hundred. She worked tirelessly, and always at the end of the day, she would light a lamp and go round the wards to see everybody herself: because of this she became known as 'the Lady of the Lamp'. Ask mum or dad if you can have a look at a £10 note; on the back you will see a picture of her with her little light shining on one of the wards of her hospital.

So successfully did Florence and her nurses help the wounded soldiers in their care that people came to see the value of good nursing and clean hospitals. By the end of her lifetime, she had made nursing one of the most respected of all professions. We owe her much.

Matthew 25: 37–40

Dear Father,
Bless all those who care for us

when we are sick:
All nurses, doctors, and other medical workers.
Help them to know that you are with them.
And help us to value what they do.

IT'S BETTER TO LIGHT A CANDLE. . . .

The vicarage sitting room was packed out with the men of
the parish, and the hubbub was tremendous. This was the
first meeting of the new men's group, so everyone was hard
at work, with the vicar as chairman, arguing out what form
their meetings should take. On one point they were all
firmly agreed: the new group mustn't be allowed to be just a
talking-shop — they were determined actually to do things,
not just to talk about them.

The Vicar's wife had been banished to the kitchen, since
the men had taken over the sitting-room. She was doing the
ironing, with one eye on the television set which had been
moved out onto the kitchen table for her to watch as she
worked.

Soon she found the programme so interesting that she put
down her iron to watch it. This was the year 1967, and the
programme was about the terrible plight of the children
made orphans by the war in Vietnam, where a bitter battle
was being fought out at that time.

She was so moved by the pictures of abandoned babies and
deserted children that she told the men all about it when she
took them coffee half way through their meeting: 'Isn't
there something we could do for them?' she asked. There
was a silence. Then one man said doubtfully, 'But there are

millions like that all over the world. There's nothing we can do.' 'Let's not be put off by the millions,' urged the vicar's wife, 'Let's try and rescue just one.'

The men thought about this for a moment or two, and then the idea began to catch fire in their minds. 'That's it!' somebody said, 'That's our project. We'll bring an orphan over here from Vietnam and find him a home and new parents.' Everyone agreed enthusiastically, and they sat down to plan the details.

That snap decision, taken over a cup of coffee, blossomed out in time to become an organisation called 'Project Vietnam Orphan'. When the war in Vietnam ended, it changed its name to 'Christian Outreach' and today it is still at work helping orphans and refugees in South East Asia.

Jesus never wasted time wringing his hands about the terrible state the whole world is in: instead, he went out and helped one person in need. It's always better to light a candle than to grumble about the dark.

Mark 8: 1–8

Lord Jesus,
Help us to feel what hurts other people, and to be sorry.
But help us not simply to feel sorry,
without also doing something to help,
as you have taught us to do.

KIDNAPPED

Where's your favourite stretch of seaside? Probably there's a particular beach or some grassy headland over towering cliffs which sticks in your memory. Of course, there can be dangers on the coast — getting carried out to sea, perhaps, or falling down a cliff face: but there's one danger you won't have to face today, and that's pirates!

And yet it wasn't always like that. There was once a lad who went wandering along the shore one evening. Suddenly, some rough-looking men ran out from behind the rocks, and in a few minutes the lad found himself hustled on board a small sailing ship drawn up on the beach.

The boy's name was Patrick, and the men were Irish pirates. All this happened a long while ago, about the year AD 400. The pirates, after they'd snatched Patrick on the English coast, sailed away with him to Ireland where they sold him as a slave. Eventually, after some time, Patrick, now a young man, escaped to France. He had grown up to love God, and he felt the best he could do would be to become a monk. But he never forgot his time in Ireland, and, before many years had passed, he was back there, spreading the Christian faith in what was then a heathen country. He was made bishop, and spent the rest of his life battling against all sorts of evil ways and beliefs, and leading people into the light of Christ. Now the Irish look back to Patrick as their patron saint, the man who brought the faith to their land.

In Patrick's adventurous life, he was often in danger but always claimed God's protection against evil. His prayer — known as 'St Patrick's Breastplate' — shows us how he did this.

Ephesians 6: 10–18

I bind unto myself today
    The power of God to hold and lead,

His eye to watch, his might to stay,
  His ear to hearken to my need;
The wisdom of my God to teach,
  His hand to guide, his shield to ward,
The word of God to give me speech,
  His heavenly host to be my guard.

OUR FEARS AND OUR FAITH

What colour's your hair? Is it dark black? Or brown and mousey? Or a corn-coloured yellow? If it's blond, then this story's specially for you!

Once upon a time, a man met a group of boys and girls, all of whom were fair-haired and blue-eyed. The place was Rome, the year was AD 585, and the man's name was Gregory; he was soon to become the Pope of Rome. He was standing in a market place at the time he met the youngsters. Now you've probably visited a market, and seen pens full of cows and sheep. This market was different, for in the pens were not pigs but people. It was a slave-market, and the boys and girls were a batch of young slaves recently brought to Rome from what was then a wild country on the very fringe of the civilised world — Britain.

Gregory, on his walk through the market, was very sad to see all these poor people who had had their freedom stolen away from them. He was particularly sorry to see the little group of English youngsters, and he was fascinated too, because he had never before met anyone from that country or seen such colouring of hair and eyes.

'Who are they?' he asked, 'they are so very fair.'

'They're Angles (for 'Angles' was what they called

English people in those days), replied his companion, 'they come from a far-off land in the north called Angle-land.'

'Surely,' said Gregory, 'they're not Angles, but angels!'

From this chance meeting in the slave market, great things were to follow. Gregory became very interested in England and the people who lived there. When he became Pope, he decided to send missionaries to spread the good news of the Christian faith to them, as this was the best way he could help.

So Pope Gregory chose a priest, Augustine, and told him to gather a band of fellow-priests to go as missionaries to Britain. Unfortunately, Augustine was not so keen on leaving the Italian sunshine for the cold and uncivilised north, with all its dangers. So he took his time and went as slowly as he could. He even stopped when he'd reached France, and wrote back to the Pope in Rome, asking him if he really had to go ahead with his formidable task. But a firm answer was sent to him, telling him to go straight ahead. So, in fear and trembling, he crossed the English Channel, certain that he was about to meet his end.

To his absolute amazement, when he'd landed on the coast he'd dreaded so much, a messenger was waiting to invite him to the palace of the local King. The palace was at Canterbury, and, when he got there, he discovered that the Queen was already a Christian; she and many of the people welcomed him warmly. Before long, Augustine had been made to feel quite at home. The people he'd feared so much turned out to be friendly after all. Soon many became Christians, and eventually Augustine was made the first Archbishop of Canterbury.

God can use even timid people for his work, if only they're willing to go forward in obedience and faith.

Matthew 28: 18–20

Dear Father God,
We thank you for Augustine,
who, though he was frightened,
went forward in faith.
Help us, when we're scared,
to go on trusting you
and doing what we know to be right.

ONE MAN'S DREAM

Fifty years ago a young man and his sister were strolling on holiday down a sunny Devon lane leading to the sea. They passed a large hotel with a wonderful view along the coast, and they stopped for a moment to read the price-list beneath the sign which announced this to be the Lee Abbey Hotel. 'One thing is certain,' said the young man — a clergyman — 'We'll never be able to afford a stay there: it's far too expensive.'

Ten years passed. The Second World War came, and in 1940 a boys' boarding school moved away from the London area and took over the now empty hotel, where it stayed for the next five years. No doubt you look after your school building carefully and treat it with respect, but, when finally the school moved out again at the end of the war, this building was left in a bad state of repair. There it stood, a depressing ruin.

But the young clergyman had never forgotten his walk down the Devon lane and his first sight of that great building with its magnificent view of the sea. He had a dream that

people, after a long and terrible war, would want somewhere to go to find peace and a restful holiday, with a chance
to discover God and his love. So he gathered some friends
together and shared his ideas with them. They had very little
money with which to buy and repair the vast property, but
they prayed tht God would show them the way, if that's
what he wanted them to do. And that is exactly what
happened.

Today, Lee Abbey is one of the biggest Christian centres
in England. Over sixty people, men and women, young and
old, married and single, run the great house and the estate
and more than 5,000 visitors come every year for holidays
and conferences, to enjoy the lovely scenery, to rest and
relax, and to find the peace of God. Many of them discover
for the first time what the Christian faith is really all about,
and come to share it.

Great things happen when God gives a person a dream of
what can be done, and that person is willing to do it.

Luke 5: 1–11

Lord God,
Help us to see your loving purpose
for us and for all men.
Help us to be willing
to be a part of your great plan,
so that, whatever we do,
we may be effective in helping others.

LITTLEST AND LEAST

What's the lowest you've ever come in your class? Probably you've never done so badly that you were placed fifty-third. But that's what happened once to a girl called Gladys Aylward, in a school in a poor area of London back in the 1920s.

She didn't do well at school, her family had little money, and to make it worse she was so tiny that the other boys and girls laughed at her. It looked as if she was fated to be a loser all her life.

As she grew into her teens she came to share her parents' staunch Christian faith, and a very curious ambition began to grow inside her: she wanted to become a missionary, to work in China, helping people and spreading the Christian faith.

Gladys Aylward studied very hard for several years, only to be turned down as her work just wasn't good enough. However, she heard of a missionary lady in China who needed someone younger to help her. So she worked hard cleaning houses to earn enough money to go, and, incredibly, managed to scrape together the fare for the cheapest possible route to China. This was by train all the way across Europe and through Russia.

At last she reached China, that vast land where one quarter of the world's population live. Even more amazingly, she managed to find the missionary lady who needed help. She lived in a large and dusty house, but Gladys soon had a wonderful plan. Together they turned the old house into a clean, bright, inn — the Inn of Eight Happinesses. Here they put up travellers, and Gladys, who now spoke the language perfectly, would tell stories about Jesus to an eager audience. Gladys became liked and trusted by all her Chinese neighbours.

Everything went well with the missionaries, until war came to China — war with the Japanese. Towns were bombed, families made homeless, and children orphaned. Gladys gathered around her a group of children and set off with them on a long walk to safety, outside the war area. Everywhere she went she gathered more children, until she'd become the leader of a long column of little Chinese boys and girls — all of whom had lost their mothers and fathers. They passed through terrible dangers, and often Gladys feared for their safety, but always her faith held her up. Eventually, after weeks of walking, she was able to deliver all her children to safe keeping.

It wasn't until after World War 2, when she'd spent twenty years working in China, that Gladys was able to come back to England and see her parents once again. To her surprise, she was famous; there was even a film made about her life.

The little woman, who'd once done so badly at school, and had been turned down by the missionaries, had become one of the best-known missionaries of all time.

1 Corinthians 1: 26–27

Dear Lord Jesus,
You use some surprising people for your work —
not the clever or the rich or the powerful,
but the simple and the poor and the weak —
anyone who's prepared to trust you.
Show us how you can use us
and teach us to trust you.

PERIL IN THE CHURCH PORCH

When did you last feel really scared at the thought of doing something or going somewhere? Perhaps you didn't want to go out into the school playground in the lunch break, because of some big bully out there. Or possibly you were frightened to go to the swimming baths because you knew someone would ask you to dive in off the top board. Or maybe they just wanted you to give the bunch of flowers to the important visitor at school prize-giving, and you hate being out in front of everyone's gaze.

If you can remember moments like these, then here's some good news for you: adults get that same butterflies-in-the-tummy feeling too. It's not only when you're young that you feel like that.

Take Sara, for instance. Sara lives in Juba in the Southern Sudan. She's a mum, with some children who've now grown up. In the 1960s when her children were small, there was a terrible civil war in that country. The army from the north were trying to track down armed bands of fighters in the south, who hid in the thick scrubland called 'the bush', from where they could attack the army and then run away to safety. Most of the southerners were Christians, while the men in the northern army were not. So the soldiers used to suspect the people in the churches of being against them, and of helping the armed bands in the bush. Sometimes the soldiers did horrible things, like shooting unarmed and harmless people, because they thought they were enemies.

Sara is a good Christian lady, and she hated all the fighting and killing. Naturally she was anxious about her family. One day a friend came to warn her that the soldiers were going to surround her church next Sunday during the morning service, and that there was going to be trouble. So Sara decided she would stay at home for once, and not go to church.

When Sunday morning came, and people began walking off to church, Sara stayed behind and started making the lunch. But a little voice inside her kept on saying — 'Why aren't you at church, Sara? That's where you should be.' After a little while Sara couldn't stand it any longer and hurried off to join her friends.

When she got there, the great thatched church was packed, and all seemed to be well. The hymns were especially joyful, backed up, not by an organ, but by a little orchestra with drums and stringed instruments. There was also sort of loud-hailer, like a wooden trumpet, through which you could chant the words to make them louder. The singing was tremendous, but even so, during the last hymn, they could hear, above the sound, the roar of trucks outside. The soldiers had arrived.

In great fear, the congregation hurried to the doorway to escape, only to find the building surrounded by soldiers, heavily armed with machine-guns. It looked as if everyone was going to be killed.

Then Sara did a very brave thing. She picked up the loud-hailer and walked out into the church porch with it. Then she spoke to the soldiers, coolly and calmly, telling them that those inside the church were harmless people, who had come there simply to worship God. God was a God of love, who wanted everyone to live together in peace, as brothers and sisters.

After Sara had spoken for some minutes, the soldiers started sheepishly scrambling to their feet and climbing back into their lorries, despite the orders of their officers. Soon the trucks drove away, though later on some of the soldiers came back, without their guns, to hear more about this God of love.

Sara had been very scared, but in the end she did what she knew she had to do, and God gave her the strength and courage to do it.

John 14: 27

Dear Father,
You know that sometimes we feel scared
to do what we should.
Give us the courage to overcome our fears,
and help us to know that you are always with us.

TRUE VALOUR

Do you ever get discouraged? Are there times when your schoolwork seems much too hard to do? Or when you think you'll never learn to swim properly, or to play tennis?

All of us get times when things are hard, and everyone seems to be against us. Then comes the acid test of our courage; do we go forward, or do we run away?

There was one man who had more than his fair share of difficulties and opposition. One of the sad things about the history of the various Christian Churches is the way that, at different times in the past, they've had wars and feuds amongst themselves. So, during this man's lifetime, 300 years ago, the laws of England were against you if you belonged to any Church other than the Church of England.

The man's name was John Bunyan, and he belonged to an Independent Church in which he was a preacher. He lived at Bedford, and he felt it right to break the laws which forbade him to preach. And so he was arrested and put into prison, and there he was to remain for the next twelve years.

What would you do if you were condemned to twelve years in prison? Would you get downhearted and discouraged? Or would you get on top of things and use the time well?

Bunyan used his long spell in prison to write books. In his lifetime he wrote some sixty Christian books, but the one by which he is best known is one he wrote in prison — 'Pilgrim's Progress'. It is the heroic story of how a man called 'Christian' goes on his pilgrimage to find God, and has to overcome every obstacle and discouragement, before finally he reaches the Celestial City. It was really, in a way, the story of his own life, and the poem in his book about Christian's triumph over difficulties could be about John Bunyan himself —

> 'Who would true valour see,
>   Let him come hither;
> One here will constant be,
>   Come wind, come weather;
> There's no discouragement;
> Shall make him once relent
> His first avowed intent
>   To be a pilgrim.'

John 16: 33

Dear Lord Jesus,
Help us when we're discouraged and depressed.
Keep us from running away and from giving up.
Strengthen us to keep on going,
just as you did,
to the very end.

ONE PAIR OF HANDS

Take a look at your hands: what are they like? Have you got long, slender fingers, or short, stubby ones? Are your nails in good shape, or broken and cracked? Are your hands clean, or a bit grubby? Whatever they're like, they are the most precious instruments you've got: just try living for one day with your hands tied behind your back, and you'll soon discover how helpless you are without them.

Hands are very precious, and so are the eyes with which you're looking at your hands.

This thought flashed through the mind of a young Indian girl called Mary Verghese. She was lying in great pain in a hospital bed, just recovering from a terrible road accident. She'd been travelling with a party of friends in a station waggon, coming back from a happy day's holiday outing. Suddenly a near collision caused the waggon to leave the road and roll over and over down a bank. Everybody in it was hurt, but Mary worst of all. She broke her jaw and nearly lost one eye, but worst of all, she damaged her spinal cord (the important nerve which runs down through your backbone): she was paralysed from the waist downwards, and would never walk again.

Mary's first thoughts, as she came back to consciousness in the hospital bed, were about her hands and her eyes. She was a student doctor, training to be a surgeon at the Christian Medical College at Vellore; it was the use of her hands and her eyesight that would be essential for her if she was to continue with her career.

She was a person of great courage and strength, and bit by bit she fought her way back to health. Eventually, she was allowed out of bed, and, though she couldn't walk, she could move about in a wheelchair. So she was able to complete her surgeon's training and to become fully qualified.

But what sort of operations can you carry out if you can't stand up? Mary learnt to specialise in an operation to help India's many leprosy patients. Sufferers from this disease frequently lose the use of their hands, because of damage to the nerves of the body. An operation was developed that could enable patients once again to use their precious hands. In time Mary became expert in performing this operation, from her wheelchair, with the patient's hand stretched out before her on a low table.

What could have been an utter tragedy for that young medical student was turned instead, through her courageous faith, into a victory over suffering and a source of blessing for many people with leprosy.

1 *Corinthians* 10: 13

Dear Lord,
We pray for all who through accident or illness,
suffer from severe handicaps;
for those who cannot walk, or see, or use their hands.
We give thanks for the faith and courage of people like Mary,
who rise above their difficulties,
to live full and useful lives.
Help us to value our skills and gifts,
and to use them
for others and for you.

DANGEROUS MOMENTS

What's the scariest moment you've ever experienced? Perhaps you've climbed a tree and got yourself stuck on the top branch, and said to yourself, 'How on earth am I going to get out of this?' Or maybe you've got an inflatable dinghy and have stupidly let yourself be blown further out from the shore than you should have done. 'How will I ever get back safe and sound to the beach?' It is at times like these when we need to say our prayers and to keep a cool head.

Of course, bad moments like that don't just hit single individuals but can come to whole nations. One such crisis occurred in 1940 during World War 2. The German army, well-equipped and highly trained, had swept across France, driving back the French and the British towards the Channel coast. It became clear that France was lost. The only question left was this — what was going to happen to the British army, now cut off, with their backs to the sea?

Many thousands of British, and many Frenchmen too, found themselves trapped in the seaside town of Dunkirk. They were surrounded by German soldiers and tanks. It looked as if it was only a matter of time before the British army would have to surrender, and then there would have been nobody left to stop Hitler's forces, if they were to cross the Channel to invade England. It was certainly a frightening moment.

However, back in England, a lot of people were busy. A great fleet of ships and craft of all sorts was brought together at great speed and sent across the Channel to bring back the troops. River steamers, coastal trading ships, motor launches, holiday ferry boats, and private yachts — all were used for this desperate escape plan. Soon a great procession of ships of all types set out across the twenty-five miles of sea to Dunkirk.

When they reached the French coast, a great difficulty met them: how were they to take off the men? Thousands of soldiers were spread out across the sands, but the ships, to avoid running aground, had to stand far out from the shore.

One of the senior officers in charge of the escape spoke to an engineer officer about this problem, and he came up with a good idea. Behind the beaches were parked hundreds of abandoned army lorries. Quickly he got together some drivers, and told them what to do. The trucks were started up, and, according to orders, driven as fast as possible into the sea, to get as far as they could before the engines cut out. Soon, lines of lorries stretched out towards the anchored ships, and the soldiers, by climbing along their canopies, could get far enough out into the sea for the ships' boats to pick them up.

The plan had worked, and, thanks to it, thousands of men got safely away during the days that were left. Every morning, the two officers, who were deeply committed Christians, called together their friends for prayer. These precious minutes which were spent in God's presence each morning gave strength and courage, to those who shared in them, for the days that remained until the last ship was able to leave, packed out with soldiers. Most of the army had escaped: Britain — and freedom — were safe. The prayers of very many people had been answered.

Exodus 14: 21–22

Father,
Jesus knew dangerous and frightening moments,
and he prayed to you in his need.
Help us, when we are scared and frightened,
to pray to you,
and then to act bravely and sensibly
as Jesus did.

STICKABILITY

What do you do when you come up against snags in some piece of work you're tackling? Suppose you're building a model plane, and somehow the pieces just won't fit together, and the longer and harder you try the more tired and cross you become. Do you grit your teeth and go on, pack up and watch television, or take a rest and come back to it later?

When things get like that, it's a great test of your 'stickability': that's the quality that keeps you going on when other people give up. It's a quality that you can see in many of the great saints — people whose faith gave them that extra bit of toughness and endurance.

Take, for instance, Teresa of Avila. She was a Spanish nun about four hundred years ago, and for most of her life she spent all her time going round opening up new nunneries where people could serve God in that particular way. She was tireless in travelling around the rugged mountain country of Spain, and no difficulties could stop her.

One day her journey was particularly rough and difficult: after a terrible time bouncing along in the ox-cart she came at last towards evening to her destination. Only one obstacle remained — a mountain stream — normally quiet and shallow, but swollen at this time with rain. Half way across it, the ox-cart stuck and would go no further. This was almost too much for Teresa.

'Lord', she prayed aloud, 'do you always treat your friends like this?'

'Yes, always, Teresa,'she heard a voice say to her.

'Then, Lord,' she answered, 'that explains why you have so few friends!'

She felt better after saying that, and with another crack of the whip she at last managed to get her ox-team moving once more, till finally she emerged onto dry land.

Teresa not only had great 'stickability'; she also kept very close to God in prayer, and she herself wrote many beautiful prayers. One of them is given below.

Romans 12: 11–12

Lord Jesus,
teach us that you have
   no body now on earth but ours,
   no hands but ours,
   no feet but ours.
Ours are the eyes through which
your compassion must look out upon the world.
Ours are the feet with which
you must go about doing good;
Ours are the hands with which
you must bless men now.

FINISHING THE JOB

What are you like at getting a job finished? Whether it's constructing a model aeroplane or making a dress, a lot of us get just so far and then we're stuck: it's too hard, or too boring, to go on, so we walk away from it and leave the task unfinished. We know that really we ought to carry it right through to the end, but somehow we just can't make it.

If you go walking on Dartmoor, about ten miles north of the city of Plymouth you'll come across a reminder of one of the greatest finishers of all time. It's a stone channel, painstakingly built of blocks, six feet wide with walls two foot high. Today it's dry but once it was an aqueduct, carrying water smoothly across the lovely countryside. It runs all of seventeen miles, and for three-hundred years it used to carry enough water from an upland river to supply the needs of the people of Plymouth.

That remarkable little channel is linked, suprisingly enough, with intrepid exploration, fabulous treasures of gold and precious stones, and with a sea-battle that changed world history. And the link is Sir Francis Drake, who amongst all his great achievements found time, while Lord Mayor of Plymouth, to make sure of the city's water supply in this way.

Whatever Sir Francis tackled he carried through to the end. In one of his voyages of discovery he reached the Isthmus of Panama — that narrow little thread of land which joins North America to South America. From a mountain top, he was able to gaze out at the Pacific Ocean, which at that time was used by Spanish ships alone and was barred to all others. Sir Francis prayed that God would let him 'sail once in an English ship in that sea'.

Sure enough, four years later, he was back with a fleet of five little vessels. Eventually, his ship alone, the *Golden Hind*, sailed round the southernmost point of South America, into the Pacific Ocean. Not content with that, he went on travelling westwards until eventually, in the year 1580, he sailed back into Plymouth Harbour, and thus became the first captain ever to sail his own ship right around the world.

Queen Elizabeth showed her pleasure by knighting him, and then, eight years later, making him her vice-admiral, when the Spaniards had gathered a fleet to attack England. It was through Drake's skill and courage that this great fleet, the Armada, was eventually defeated and destroyed. Once again, Sir Francis had finished the job.

So, the next time you're tempted to give up, just remember Sir Francis Drake, and then keep going. Sir Francis was a great Christian, and he knew that Jesus, faced with a terrible course that would lead him to his death on the cross, nevertheless had seen it through, right to the end. No doubt that's what inspired Sir Francis to keep going in the teeth of danger and difficulty, and to compose the following prayer, all about finishing what you begin.

John 19: 28–30

O Lord God,
When thou givest to thy servants to endeavour any great matter,
grant us also to know that it is not the beginning
but the continuing of the same, until it be thoroughly finished,
which yieldeth the true glory;
through him who, for the finishing of thy work,
laid down his life for us,
our Redeemer, Jesus Christ.

THE MAN IN A HURRY

What would you do if you were being given some homework, and, by pure mistake, the master set you twice as much to do as he'd intended? Would you do only half, and make a tremendous fuss the next day about the mistake? Or would you grit your teeth and tackle the lot?

There was once a man who had to face a rather similar decision. His name was George Augustus Selwyn, and in the year 1841 the Church of England sent him out to be their first Bishop of New Zealand. Unfortunately, there was a very big mistake in the letter appointing him to the post: in describing the area of which he was to be the Bishop, the clerk had written 'Northern Latitude', where he should have written 'Southern Latitude'. The effect of this stupid mistake was to make Selwyn Bishop not only of New Zealand — an enormous area in itself — but also of the Melanesian Islands in the Pacific Ocean, stretching nearly 4,000 miles to the north.

If it had been you, would you have complained, or would you have taken on this enormous task? Bishop Selwyn, a man of great energy, decided to accept responsibility for the whole vast region, half of it given to him in error!

You can judge what sort of a man he was by the fact that he learnt the language of the Maoris, the native inhabitants of New Zealand, while he was still on the ship out from England, so that, as soon as he stepped ashore, he was able to preach straight away to Maoris as well as to English people. He wasted no time in visiting his enormous diocese, travelling on foot through both the Islands of New Zealand, and sailing to the scattered communities of the Pacific in his own schooner (he'd learnt navigation as well, before leaving home).

He was so impatient to get on with the job that he sometimes went too fast for those around him. At the school he set up for Maoris and English boys, he made a rule that the midday meal had to be eaten in just ten minutes, and it wasn't until everybody got indigestion and complained that he relaxed the rule and gave them longer.

Nevertheless, his restless energy meant that, in the space

of just twenty-six years as Bishop, he'd managed to appoint clergymen, build churches and schools, and split up his vast diocese into more manageable areas. He also tried hard to protect the Maoris against unfair treatment by the white settlers. He set himself rules for living his life: here are a couple —

'What is worth doing is worth doing well.'

'Do all to the glory of God.'

If our work is really important to us, then it's worth all the time and all the energy we can give to it. Bishop Selwyn believed in spreading the Christian message and the Christian way of life, and just like the first great missionary, St Paul, he spared nobody — least of all himself — to carry this task forward.

Romans 12: 6–11

Lord Jesus,
We thank you for the example of men like Bishop Selwyn,
who work hard because their task is urgent.
Help us to find the work that we can do best,
and to do it well, for your glory.

FLEEING TO FREEDOM

What's the longest journey you've ever made? Perhaps you've travelled for hours by car, or rattled through the night in a train? Or maybe you've covered hundreds of miles through the sky in an airliner? Or have you experienced a sea voyage, in some large and comfortable passenger ship?

One thing's certain: you will not have spent eight weeks fighting the mountainous waves of the Atlantic Ocean in a little sailing ship just 90 feet long. Yet that's just what a heroic little group of people were prepared to do, back in the year 1620.

They were English people, but they wanted to get away from England so that they could start a new life in a new land — America. At that time everybody in England had to worship God in just one way — the Church of England way: otherwise the law made life very difficult for you. Many people didn't like this, and wanted to work out a new way of worshipping God for themselves. As they saw it, they wanted to make religion more pure, so they were called 'Puritans'.

So strongly did these Puritans want to be free that they were willing to risk their lives on a tiny ship for a chance of finding freedom. Of their two ships, one sprang a leak right at the start, so that in the end they all crowded into the other little vessel, the 'Mayflower'. Besides the crew, there were 102 men and women, boys and girls squeezed into its hold.

Somehow they managed the long crossing, and landed near where the city of Boston now stands. In the cold winter that followed, half of them died: yet somehow the heroic little group — known later as the Pilgrim Fathers — hung on and built the new, free, life for which they had suffered so much.

Freedom — being free to do the important things your way — is worth a lot. God wants us to be free, free from the bullying of others and free also from everything from within ourselves that can spoil our lives.

Galatians 5: 1

Lord Jesus,
We thank you for all those
who have been willing to suffer,
so as to be free.
Free us from all that shuts us in
and spoils our lives.
And help us to enjoy our freedom.

REAL FREEDOM

Where did King John sign the Magna Carta?

'On Runnymede' — not bad.

'At the bottom' — even better.

Actually, you're both wrong, because he didn't sign it at all: he simply fixed his seal to it. And he didn't sign it for the simple reason that he didn't know how to read and write. In those days, if you were really important you didn't bother to learn how to read. You left all that sort of thing to your clerks, who looked after all the small print for you, leaving you to do more important things, like going out hunting.

Signed or not, Magna Carta is a very important document because it was the first time that some valuable rights and freedoms were actually written down and agreed. The most important right set down in Magna Carta is the right not to be put in prison unless people have been properly tried before a law-court and found guilty. So it's quite a landmark in the history of freedom (and you don't need to be reminded that all this was as long ago as 1215). That's why the few precious copies of Magna Carta are looked after with such care, so that many thousands of people can come and read it.

Another important document that sets out people's right to freedom is the Declaration of Independence, signed in 1776 by the leaders of the American States who were then at war with Britain, fighting to break away from British rule. This Declaration, preserved very carefully in Washington, makes great claims in some splendid words — 'We hold these truths to be self-evident, that all men are created equal, that they are endowed by their Creator with certain rights; that among these are life, liberty, and the pursuit of happiness'.

So precious is this paper that it is kept locked up in a special case above a deep shaft dropping down into the earth: this is so that, if there were ever a war and there were to be a nuclear bomb on Washington, this document could be lowered rapidly underground, where it would be kept safe from any damage.

These are two valuable documents that have helped to set people free, each of them treasured with great care. But there is another piece of paper that's been even more help in freeing people, and this you can find, not locked up in a glass case, but on the bookshelf in every home. Of course, it's the Bible, the book that tells us about Jesus, who came to set us all free from selfishness, from lies, from bad temper and from everything else that can spoil our lives.

Romans 8: 1–2

Lord Jesus,
We thank you for the way brave men have fought for freedom,
and we thank you for documents like Magna Carta
and the Declaration of Independence,

which reflect their victories.
But even more we thank you for the Bible,
which tells us about you
who came to set us free to live better lives.

A BOOK WORTH READING

What's the furthest you've ever walked? Maybe you've taken part in a sponsored walk to raise money for some good cause, and perhaps you notched up ten miles or so. Or perhaps you've got a dog that needs exercising, so that you cover mile after mile pounding the pavement, or exploring the park. Or possibly you all go walking as a family when you're away on holiday, up on the hills or along a coastal path.

You've probably never tackled on foot a round trip of fifty miles — twenty-five miles out one day, and twenty-five back the next. You'd really need to want something badly to be prepared to walk that far for it. And yet that's exactly what one young girl was prepared to do.

Her name was Mary Jones and she lived 200 years ago on the wild coastline of North Wales. Her parents weaved cloth in their little cottage, and they didn't have much money to spare. In those days that part of Wales was very remote, and all sorts of things we would take for granted just couldn't be found there. There was, for example, no school when Mary reached the age to go to one, and she had to wait several years before people got together to build one.

This meant Mary was ten years old before she was able to learn to read. She was impatient to learn, because there was one book she really wanted to read, and that book was the

Bible. Even when she'd learnt, she had no Bible of her own: people in that area spoke Welsh, and Welsh Bibles were rare and expensive. So, every Saturday, Mary would walk two miles up the valley to the house of a kindly farmer's wife, who owned a Bible and was happy to let her study it.

Mary wanted a Bible of her very own, so she began to save up to buy one. Now, if you want something really badly, *you* can probably collect enough money together in just a few weeks to get it: Mary had to go on saving for six years. Even then her troubles were not over. The nearest person who could sell her a Bible was a clergyman, a Revd. Williams, but he lived twenty-five miles away. Nevertheless, Mary thought it was worth the effort, so she set out on her great walk. When she arrived, Mr Williams was touched by her determination and gave her the Bible she wanted. So, on his next visit to London, he spoke to a meeting of Christian people from different churches and told them all about Mary Jones, and what it had cost her to have a Bible in her own language.

The Revd. Williams' story really got through, and the meeting decided to set up a new society to print and publish the Bible not only in Welsh but in as many different languages as they possibly could; in this way people the world over would have the chance to read the Bible's message. That decision was the start of the Bible Society, which today has actually produced Bibles in almost every known language.

All this happened because Mary Jones was so keen to have a Bible that she was prepared to walk fifty miles to get one.

Psalm 119: 105

Dear Lord,
People like Mary Jones have found the Bible so precious

that they were prepared to give everything to have it.
Help us to discover for ourselves
what they found in its pages,
and to treasure its message for ourselves.

PAINTING THE CEILING

Do you enjoy art lessons? Drawing perhaps, or using cray-
ons and charcoal, or painting in oil paint, acrylics, or water
colour? It so, do you prefer drawing people or things?
What's the largest picture you have ever done? Perhaps you
stay with pictures that will fit comfortably onto a large sheet
of paper: but maybe you've ventured out and done something bigger — a painting on a large canvas, perhaps, or even
on a wall.

One thing's very certain, though — you won't ever have
painted a whole ceiling. And yet that's exactly what one of
the world's greatest artists set out to do some 400 years ago.
His name was Michelangelo, and he was an Italian. At that
time the Pope in Rome was building a new chapel, and he
wanted the ceiling specially decorated, so he sent for
Michelangelo, an up-and-coming young artist from the city
of Florence. He not only agreed to tackle the task but took
the Pope's plans and made them better.

To paint the ceiling he had to lie on his back, on a wooden
platform specially made for the purpose. And that's what
Michelangelo began to do one day in 1508. Four years later
he finished the task: it had taken him all that time working
day by day flat on his back. You can imagine how stiff his
muscles became. For a long time afterwards, even to read a
letter, he had to hold it above his head and look up at it. But

it was worth it: he had created a masterpiece — a whole ceiling filled with figures of great power, full of life and movement. You can see it for yourself if you have the chance to go to Rome and visit the Sistine Chapel.

Michelangelo wasn't only a painter. He was also an architect, and, above all, a sculptor. He liked to look at a great block of marble, and imagine a human figure inside it, trying to break out and escape. When he set about a carving, he felt he was just setting free the figure that was already there, locked up inside the stone.

Jesus, too, was always setting people free. He'd come and see somebody trapped and shut in by disease or by their own wrong deeds, and he'd let them out to become what God had always meant them to be. For Jesus was a craftsman even greater than Michelangelo.

Luke 19: 1–10

Lord Jesus,
Thank you for artists
who can look at what is there
and see what it might become.
Please look at our lives.
Free us from all that holds us back.
So that we can become
what you would have us be.

TRUE GREATNESS

Does your mum ever have one of those disasters in the kitchen, when something she's been cooking has been allowed to stay on the stove too long and gets burnt? Then you have clouds of smoke, no cakes for tea, and burnt saucepans to wash up.

Do you know the story about a king who let some cakes burn? You've probably heard how King Alfred, a great and wise king who ruled over the west of England eleven hundred years ago, was once travelling alone across his kingdom. When night fell, he knocked at the door of a little cottage and asked the lady who lived there if he might stay the night. She did not know who he was, but she let him in and told him to watch over the cakes she was cooking while she prepared his bedroom. But the king was tired from his journey, and worried about the war he was fighting against the Danish invaders of his land. Quite soon, worn out with his problems, he fell asleep and so the cakes were burned. The lady of the house, when she saw what had happened, got very cross with him and was telling him off when there came another knock at the door; it was one of Alfred's nobles, who had followed him with urgent news. You can imagine how the woman felt when she discovered that it was the king whom she had been scolding.

Eventually, Alfred won his war against the Danes, and not only made peace throughout England, but also, because he was a great Christian, persuaded the Danes, who were pagans, to learn all about Christianity and to accept it.

If you go today to Winchester, which was once Alfred's capital, you can see there a great statue of the king who was humble enough to let himself be scolded, but great enough to bring peace to his kingdom. During his reign he did many good things — built our first fleet of ships, started our system of law, translated books from Latin into English, and encouraged his nobles to learn to read. But perhaps the finest thing he ever did was to spread the teachings of Jesus throughout the land, so that peace and law and learning could flourish. That is why he alone, of all our kings, is called 'the Great'.

Matthew 5: 6–9

Dear Father God,
Thank you for so much
that we take for granted everyday —
the books we read,
the school we go to,
the policemen who keep law and order,
the churches we can visit.
Help us to remember
all who gave us these good things
and to be grateful.

HOW BLIND CAN YOU BE?

Have you had that tiresome experience of hunting high and low to find something, and eventually discovering it right under your nose? Then, to make it worse, someone tells you that you must be blind as a bat not to have seen it earlier.

All of us are a bit blind at times and fail to see things which are perfectly obvious to others. This doesn't matter too much if we are talking about finding a biro or a book, but suppose we are concerned with really important things, talking, for instance about not seeing what's right, even if it's quite clear to others?

Now this happens to all of us too. We have a blind spot, so that we don't realise when we are being unkind and unfair to somebody else. Sometimes this blindness can strike a whole nation, so that they can't see that they're being unfair, for instance, to people of another religion, or colour, or race.

It's terrible to think that the whole Christian Church was blind for nearly 1,800 years when it came to the subject of slavery. Church leaders and ordinary Christians alike just could not see that it was utterly wrong for one person to own another and to use his work.

People in Britain, 200 years ago, were particularly bad about this, because a lot of British shipowners were making great fortunes buying up people captured as slaves on the west coast of Africa, and then shipping them to America, to be sold for a great profit. Packed tight in the overcrowded ships, very many slaves died on the voyage. But, eventually, a small group of concerned people managed to put an end to this horrifying situation.

Chief among this group was a Member of Parliament, William Wilberforce. As a young man, it seemed that he had a lot going for him. He'd inherited a great deal of money, went to all the best parties, and knew everyone important, from the Prince of Wales downwards. A very agreeable future lay before him.

Then, one day, he picked up a book all about the Christian faith. The book really got through to William, and he saw that he must do something much more serious and worthwhile with his life. So he went to see a clergyman, John Newton. Now, as it happens, before he became a Christian, John Newton had been a sea-captain, engaged in the slave trade, but then his new-found faith had shown him how wicked the whole business was. So he urged William Wilberforce to use his influence in Parliament to fight slavery.

And that was exactly what Wilberforce went on to do. Over the next thirty years he campaigned tirelessly to have slavery made illegal. Many people were against him, and his long battle made him a most unpopular man. In 1807 he got Parliament to stop the trade in slaves, but it took another twenty-six years to have slavery itself made illegal. Eventually he succeeded, and in the year 1833 a law was passed finally freeing the slaves in all British territories — as somebody said 'One of the three or four truly good acts in human history'.

People who had been so blind about the evils of slavery had now at long last come to see just how wicked and wrong it had been. Today, we can't understand how they ever failed to see what to us is so obvious. It took a small group of determined Christian people to open everyone's eyes.

Matthew 5: 14–16

Dear Lord God,
help us to see
what is right and what is wrong.
Show us when we're being
unkind or unfair to others.
Keep us from being blind and hard-hearted.
Help us to see.

CHRIST THE PEACEMAKER

How much geography do you know? What's the name of the mountain range that forms the spine of South America?

Well, of course, you came up with the answer in a flash. If

you said 'Andes', then you were perfectly correct. Full marks!

Down towards the southern tip of the continent, the Andes range serves to separate two great nations — Chile on the west, and Argentina on the east.

For a long period — over fifty years — these two countries had a quarrel about where precisely that frontier should lie. They just could not agree about it, and on several occasions they came almost to the point of war.

Eventually, they decided to ask somebody who was not involved in the dispute to act as judge for them, to settle the matter once and for all. So they asked King Edward VII if he would help them, since the British were greatly respected in both the two countries.

King Edward at once sent a team from England to work out where the frontier should lie, but even while the team was at work on a solution to the problem, the two nations they'd come to help once more began to prepare for war. It actually reached the point where troops of the two armies had been loaded into trains, ready to take them high up into the Andes to fight it out and decide the question in battle. But at this dangerous moment, the Argentine Archbishop appealed to both governments in the name of Christ, to turn from war and accept a peaceful settlement of their quarrel. The Archbishop's appeal was heard, and, in 1902, the two countries accepted the answer proposed by the team from England.

To mark their agreement, they melted down cannon which were to have been used in the war that in the end was never fought, and from the metal was made a great statue of Christ, which stands to this day high up on that mountain frontier. At the foot of the statue the following words are carved — 'These mountains will fall before Argentines and

Chileans break the peace sworn at the feet of Christ the Redeemer'.

That promise has been kept, and there has been no war between Chile and Argentina. They called King Edward 'Edward the Peacemaker', because of the help that he had been able to give. But the real peacemaker was Christ, who puts the love of peace in men's hearts, and who gave the leaders of the two nations the will to choose peace and not war.

Ephesians 2: 13–18

Lord Jesus,
you came to show us the way to peace —
peace with you, peace with one another.
You break down our hardness and our pride,
that lead us into quarrels and fighting.
Put the love of peace in our hearts,
so that we can serve you better.

BROTHERS

It was a clear and starlit night, and the sentry as he paced slowly up and down, could make out the dark shapes of trees a hundred yards away. Despite the good visibility, the soldier was nervous, because this was a dangerous post. It was the American Civil War (1861–65) and he was serving in the Northern Army. It was known that the advance guard of the army of the Southern States was not very far away. So the sentry kept a good look-out; as he watched, he sang softly to himself, to keep up his courage. And what he sang was a hymn — 'Jesus, lover of my soul'.

Twenty years later, long after the war had ended, he was singing that same hymn once again, this time on a happier occasion. He was with a party of friends on a pleasure steamer travelling down the River Potomac from Washington. Because he had a fine voice, his friends asked him to sing for them, and he chose, once again, the same hymn.

As soon as he began to sing, another traveller on the boat looked up at him with an expression of intense suprise. When the singer had finished the stranger came up to him and asked him if he'd served in the war.

'Why, yes,' the man replied, 'I was in the Northern Army, under General Grant.' 'In that case,' said the stranger, 'I have heard you sing that hymn once before. I was in the Southern forces, and one night I was sent out to reconnoitre your front line. I saw a sentry silhouetted against the sky, and he was singing, very quietly, that same hymn. I raised my rifle and took aim, but, just as I was about to fire, you — for I recognise your voice — sang the lines:

'Cover my defenceless head
With the shadow of thy wing.'

'After that, I lowered my rifle; I just couldn't shoot.'

Jesus tells us that all men are really brothers. And he said that we mustn't so much as curse our brothers, let alone kill them.

Matthew 5: 43–48

Lord Jesus,
You want everybody to be your brother or sister.
You draw us all into one great family.
Help us to see each person we meet

as a friend and brother,
because that is what you would want,
within your family.

FROM FLAMES TO FORGIVENESS

On 13 November 1940, in World War 2, the city of Coventry was a thriving industrial centre, making cars, trucks, and weapons. A large number of people lived within sight of the city's ancient cathedral. By the 15 November, the city and the cathedral had become a flattened shambles of smoking ruins, in which many thousands of people had died. During the night a fleet of German bombers had dropped 500 tons of high explosives on Coventry.

Poking around in the Cathedral ruins the morning after the bombing, a caretaker found two charred timbers. He lashed them together in the form of a cross and stood it up against the shattered East wall. There it stood, as a reminder of the words of Jesus on the cross — 'Father, forgive them: they don't know what they're doing.'

It was to be years before the cathedral could be rebuilt, but right away the clergy and congregation began to preach the Christian message of forgiveness and healing. Soon a little group of people came into being called 'The Community of the Cross of Nails'. The group took its name from a small cross made out of three nails found in the ruins, and their aim was to show Christian love and forgiveness wherever they could. They knew that the only way to heal the terrible wounds of war was to show care and understanding in some practical way, and so to let the healing work begin. One of their first achievements, as soon as the war was over, was to build a hospital wing in Dresden, a German city which had been bombed even more terribly than Coventry.

Forgiving other people, as Jesus did, is very hard, but it's the only way to put things right and to start again.

Ephesians 4: 32 to 5: 2

Father,
It's so easy to hit back when people hurt us.
Teach us the hardest lesson of all
— how to forgive.
And if we find it tough,
help us to remember that you managed to forgive us.

THE HARDEST WORD TO SAY

What's the hardest word to say? What about 'super-calafragalisticexpialladocious'? No, that's quite easy once you've got the hang of it. What are the really difficult words that you know?

Actually, it is probably none of the best-known tongue-twisters at all. It's the word 'forgive'. There are times when we find it almost impossible to say 'I forgive'. It can be more unpronounceable than even the word 'sorry'.

This was what a Dutch lady discovered, just after World War 2. During the war, Corrie — for that was her name — and her family lived in a little house in a town called Haarlem. Here her father had a good business repairing clocks. Holland, like other European countries, was occupied by the Nazis, who soon began to take away to prison anyone who tried to resist them. Corrie's family were very brave, because they used to hide people, especially Dutch Jews, who were escaping from the enemy. They even built a false wall in the house, to conceal a little room where people could hide safely. Many people owed their lives to this brave family.

Then, one day, there came a sudden fierce knocking on the door: it was the Nazi police. They had been betrayed. The house was searched and even the hidden room was found. The family, and those they had been hiding, were taken away to prison, where they were treated very badly indeed. Corrie and her sister Betsie were eventually sent to a terrible place, where many women were emprisoned, guarded by barbed wire and men with fierce dogs. Here they all had to work hard, but they were given very little to eat. Many died, from overwork, hunger and disease.

Both Corrie and her sister were strong Christians, and their faith kept them going. They felt God was with them when they prayed, and they were able to do much to help others. Then Betsie fell ill and, to Corrie's great sorrow, died. Corrie, however, survived and was eventually released. When the war was over, she did all she could to make friends with the Germans who had been their enemies, and had done so much harm to their country.

One day Corrie was preaching in Germany about all that she had suffered, and about the need to forgive. When the service ended, she saw amongst the congregation a man whom she recognised. To her horror it was one of the guards from that terrible camp, one of those who had been so cruel to the prisoners. He came up to her, smiling all over his face, and told her how he had now become a Christian, and was sorry for what he had done. He held out his hand to shake hers, and Corrie found she just couldn't take it. It was as if her arm were paralysed. As she thought of her dead sister she simply could not forgive him for what he had done.

Then, as she stood and prayed for help, a wonderful thing happened. She felt a new power in her arm that enabled her to raise her hand and take that of the man who had once been her enemy.

God helps us to say 'I forgive', even when, by ourselves, we cannot manage to do it.

Luke 23: 32–34

Lord Jesus,
You said, 'Father forgive them . . .'
when they nailed you to the cross.
You managed it.
Give us the strength we need to say hard things
like 'I forgive', and 'I'm sorry'.

FEUDS AND FRIENDSHIPS

Who's your best friend? Is it someone you know from school, or somebody living next door to you? It's good to have a special pal you can meet after school and play with, and it's nice to be able to befriend anyone you like, who enjoys the same sort of games or shares the same interests.

Just suppose, instead, that you had to choose your friends from those in the same street; beyond that you could not go. Just suppose, too, that you weren't allowed to go about town wherever you wanted, or to enjoy the swimming pool or soccer ground, but had to stay around in your own street or your own home most of the time. And just suppose you could talk only to boys and girls from your own school. Wouldn't that be just terrible?

That's the way it is, though, for thousands of youngsters who live in Northern Ireland, where the terrible feud between the Roman Catholic and Protestant communities means that people live separate lives. People from one community live in one part of town, people from the other community in another, and it could be dangerous to leave your own area. Often the swimming baths, and the cinemas and the sportsgrounds have to be closed because of bomb scares, and altogether life can be very shut-in and difficult.

However, there are also some signs of hope. Lots of children are invited for holidays outside Northern Ireland, in Britain and elsewhere, and then they can make friends and play freely together. Better still, in Northern Ireland itself, there are big houses out in the country where people, young and old, can go and meet one another in safety. One such house is called Corrymeela, and for years now this has been a centre where people can meet and talk and get to know one another.

It's a terrible thing when people have feuds and rows, and some get hurt. When such quarrels are carried on in the name of the Christian religion it's specially bad, because Jesus himself was always bringing men together and telling them to love one another. You can only really hate people you've never met and you don't know: once you actually see them and speak to them, you find they're just like you and you can make friends with them. Jesus must be pleased with places like Corrymeela, which exist to let people meet and forgive and make friends.

Ephesians 2: 13–14

Lord Jesus,
Forgive us when we have quarrels and rows.
Help us to try and understand other people,
and to look for the best in them,
so that we can become their friends,
as you would want us to.

FEUDS IN THE FAMILY

Have you ever thought what a terrible thing it would be if everybody was exactly the same? Just suppose, for example, that every single person you met had precisely the same sort of face, just like a row of identical dolls on a shelf in a toy shop. And imagine if, when they opened their mouths, the same sound came out of each. How terribly boring that would be!

But of course it's not like that. Instead, there are short people, fat people, tall people and thin people. Some of us are brown, some black or yellow, and others of us are white. And we don't think the same way, either. We've got different ideas about what we like and what we don't like, different ideas about how the country should be run, and different ideas about God.

Now it's these differences that make life such fun, and that's how God meant it to be. It's fun to meet people from other countries, it's fun to make friends with people who don't think the same way as we do, and it's fun to find out how other people worship God.

The trouble is that there's something in us which makes

us want to look down on people who are not like ourselves. Because they're different, we say we must be better than they are. So it is that people of one colour have looked down on people of another colour, one race thinks it's better than those from other countries, and people of this religion fancy themselves better than people of that religion.

It's not so very long ago, for instance, that black people in the United States of America had to struggle for fair and just treatment from white Americans: in the past they were very unfairly treated. One of their leaders in this struggle was a black clergyman called Martin Luther King. He led his people in all sorts of peaceful ways of winning their rights — through non-violent marches and gatherings. Yet, even though he preached love for all men, white and black, some white people were bitterly against him. He received threats and insults and twice bombs were thrown at his home. But he still kept on.

One day, in a town called Memphis, he gave a great speech, in which he explained how it would be when all Americans, black and white, really did see themselves as equal brothers and sisters. It would be the sort of land that God had promised, then. This is part of what he said —

> 'I've been to the mountain top. And I've looked over, and I've seen the promised land. I may not get there with you, but I want you to know that we as a people will get to the promised land. So I'm happy tonight. I'm not worried about anything.'

The very next day Martin Luther King was shot and killed by somebody who wanted to stop what he was doing. Yet, even though he died, his cause lived on. Today, black and white people in the USA can really see themselves as different but equally valuable human beings.

After all, God is the heavenly Father of each one of us.

1 *John* 3: 15–17

Dear Father God,
Thank you for making us so different from each other,
but also for loving each one of us equally.
Help us to know that
we are all equally precious in your family,
and that no one is left out.

SUBJECT INDEX
WITH BIBLE REFERENCES